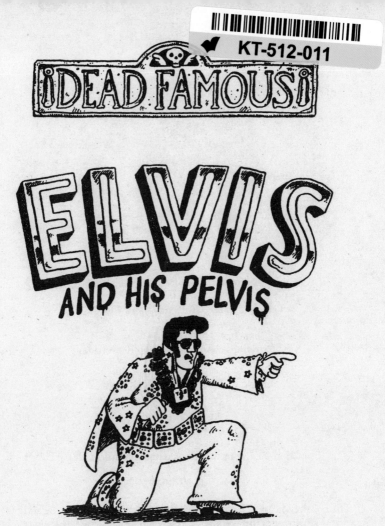

DEAD FAMOUS

ELVIS
AND HIS PELVIS

by Michael Cox

Illustrated by Philip Reeve

Hippo

Scholastic Children's Books,
Euston House, 24 Eversholt Street,
London, NW1 1DB, UK
A division of Scholastic Ltd
London ~ New York ~ Toronto ~ Sydney ~ Auckland
Mexico City ~ New Delhi ~ Hong Kong

Published in the UK by Scholastic Ltd, 2001

Text copyright © Michael Cox, 2001
Illustrations copyright © Philip Reeve, 2001

10 digit ISBN 0 439 99756 9
13 digit ISBN 978 0439 99756 0

Typeset by M Rules
Printed in the UK by CPI Bookmarque, Croydon, CR0 4TD

23 25 27 29 30 28 26 24

The right of Michael Cox and Philip Reeve to be identified as the author
and illustrator of this work respectively has been asserted by them in
accordance with the Copyright, Designs and Patents Act, 1988.

Papers used by Scholastic Children's Books are made from wood
grown in Sustainable forests.

INTRODUCTION

Even though he wiggled his last wiggle way, way back in the 1970s, almost everyone has heard of Elvis. And they know *loads* of stuff about him, like...

HE WAS MIND-BOGGLINGLY GENEROUS! HE GAVE AWAY NEW CARS TO FRIENDS AND STRANGERS!

FOOEY! HE WAS TIGHT AS A TEACHER'S TICK-STICK! HE WOULDN'T GIVE HIS BACKING BAND A RISE — HE GOT $25,000 A WEEK WHILE THEY GOT $200!

HE WAS SLIM, HANDSOME AND A MODEL OF HEALTHY LIVING! HE TOLD HIS MUM OFF FOR DRINKING BEER AND NAGGED PEOPLE TO STOP SMOKING!

BALONEY! HE WAS FAT AND HAD PLASTIC SURGERY! HE WAS ADDICTED TO JUNK FOOD AND STAYED IN BED ALL DAY!

HE WANTED TO SET A GOOD EXAMPLE FOR YOUNG PEOPLE AND MADE DONATIONS TO SCHOOLS AND CHARITIES!

HORSE FEATHERS! HE WAS A ROCK AND ROLL ROOF-RAISER! HE GOT CHUCKED OUT OF HOTELS, HAD FIGHTS AND PARTIED LIKE THERE WAS NO TOMORROW!

HEY! ARE YOU SURE WE'RE TALKING ABOUT THE SAME ELVIS?

Well yes, you are!

Elvis was *all* of these things and more. Because, like most people, he was neither completely good ... nor completely bad! However, *unlike* most people, he rocketed from being mind-bogglingly poor to mind-bogglingly rich in a couple of shakes of his famous pelvis and went on to lead a rock 'n' roll music 'n' movie-star lifestyle that had the whole world's eyes out on stalks for the next 20 years or so. And more than two decades after his death, he still regularly pops up in newspapers and magazines, still inspires loads of pop stars, and has still got an army of fans that makes other celebs green with envy.

This book is packed with stacks of sizzling stories and devastating data about the amazing King of Rock 'n' Roll, like the secret behind his famous wiggle, why girls pressed handkerchieves to their noses at his movie audition, how he started a riot with a joke, why he put 3,000 marbles in a musician's dressing room, who *his* heroes were, and how he finally toppled from his 'throne'. It also contains terrific tales of his telly-shooting tantrums, his staggering spending sprees, the luxury cars he gave away to complete strangers, and the nutty stuff his fans got up to.

You can get the lowdown on some crazy scrapes he got into with his 'gang', the Memphis Mafia, check out some of his pesky 'hillbilly' rellies, meet a few of his hundreds of girlfriends, raise an eyebrow or three at his *deeply* dodgy manager and shed a tear for his tragic mum. And you can learn how to become the best Elvis impersonator ever whilst rustling up one of his fave gut-busting 'snacks'. Finally, in addition to all that, you can get the King of Rock 'n' Roll's own side of the story, by reading what Elvis might have written in his legendary Lost Diary. So, order a couple of thousand cheeseburgers, slip on your blue suede shoes, perk up your pony-tail … and get yourself all shook up!

THAT'S RIGHT Y'ALL! LISTEN UP, YA HEAR!

ITTY-BITTY ELVIS

Elvis was born on a freezing cold night at 4.35 a.m. on 8 January 1935 in his mum and dad's wooden house in the little town of East Tupelo in the American state of Mississippi.

As well as being a great occasion for music lovers everywhere, Elvis's arrival in the world was also a very unhappy one. About half an hour earlier his twin brother, Jessie, had been born dead.

The tiny, two-roomed building that Elvis popped up in was known around those parts as a 'shotgun shack' (sort of a starter home for very small mice). In order to build it his dad, Vernon, had borrowed 180 dollars from his boss, Orville Bean. Why was it called a 'shotgun shack'? Because if you stood at the front door and fired a shotgun, the bullet would go straight in the front door and out of the back door!

The reason the Presleys lived in a shotgun shack was because they were mind-bogglingly poor! Just like almost all their Presley ancestors had been.

Them pesky Presleys' family album

Absolutely *loads* is now known about Elvis's family background because ever since he got famous all sorts of swots and nosey parkers have spent ages clambering in and out of his family tree trying to find out about the various characters he inherited his amazing rock 'n' roll genes from. In other words, there are stacks of people around now who know loads *more* about Elvis's way-back rellies than Elv' himself ever did! Elvis's dad, Vernon, knew even *less* about the Presley background than his famous son did. When someone told Vernon that his surname was British he was gob-smacked! He said he'd never heard tell of any of his kinfolk coming over from *anywhere*! He said it seemed like Presleys had *always* been there (i.e. in the good old USA!). American history obviously wasn't one of Vernon's strong subjects. Anyway, there were so many Presleys in East Tupelo where Elv' was born that at one time the school had 26 kids in it … all called Presley!

Now, it would be really *great* to tell you about every one of Elvis's amazing kinfolk.

But there just isn't room!

So instead, here are some of the *really* interesting ones:

Andrew Presley Junior (1754–1855)
Andrew was Elvis's great-times-who-cares-exactly-how-many-grandad. Even though he was called Junior, Andrew didn't turn up his toes until he was 101! He was the son of Andrew Presley Senior who came to America from Britain in 17-something or other and was just about the first *ever* Presley to come to the New World, as it used to be called. Andrew Junior fought in the American War of

Independence against the British. He claimed that during one battle with the Redcoats their musket balls actually passed through his clothing but didn't injure him. So there you are … the first ever example of the amazing swivelling Presley pelvis!

Morning Dove (1800–1835ish)
Although she sounds like a rather nice brand of hand cream, Morning Dove was actually Elvis's great-great-great-

grandma. She was a Cherokee Indian girl who married William Mansell, Elvis's great-great-great-grandaddy. In the early rough, tough pioneering days of the nineteenth century there were lots of rough, tough, grizzled European settler chaps wandering around America seeking their fortune and a gorgeous gal to share it with as soon as they'd made it, but unfortunately there weren't lots of rough, tough European women to marry them. However there were quite a few beautiful Native American girls around. So in addition to roughing up the locals and pinching their land and natural resources, the pioneers also pinched their girlfriends. And that's why Elvis was ½ Native American. Elvis once acted the role of a man who was part Native American and part white man in his film *Flaming Star*. Some film critics have said it was the best bit of acting he ever did.

WHO'S ACTING?

People also reckoned that Elvis inherited his dark eyes from his Indian ancestry.

Minnie Mae Hood Presley (1893–1980)

Minnie was Elvis's grandma on his dad's side of the family. Elvis called her Dodger because he'd once thrown a baseball bat at her and she'd dodged out of the way really niftily. (Hey, *another* nimble mover!) She was said to be really feisty (American for bouncy, with lots of vim and vinegar). She went to live with Elvis and his folks when she got divorced from her hubby in 1947. Minnie was forever taking snuff (no wonder he divorced her) and wore sunglasses nearly all the time.

She survived both Elvis and his parents but eventually snuffed it, er, passed away, at the creaky old age of 86.

Jessie Presley (1896–1973)

Jessie was Minnie's hubby and in addition to being incredibly handsome he was also said to be a bit of a lad. (Don't ask which bit.) He was also thought to be a bit of a peacock as well, and although he didn't have two American Express cards to rub together he loved to wear expensive snazzy clothes. It's said that Elvis inherited his good looks from his grandad Jessie (but not his clothes, thank goodness).

Great Uncle Noah Presley (dates unknown)

Uncle Noah was the mayor of Tupelo and drove the local kids to school in his bus (unless it was raining heavily, when he used his Ark).

He owned the grocery store too. During a day out he gave young nephew Elvis his first ever sight of Memphis, the city he would eventually return to and find fame and fortune in. This trip took place when Uncle Noah took all the Tupelo kids to the Memphis zoo in his bus (but had to take them all home again after the keepers told him they hadn't got a big enough cage for them all).

Vernon Elvis Presley (1916–1979)

Vernon was 19 when he became Elvis's dad. Just like Elvis, Vernon was also known as the 'King' ... the 'King of Lower Back Pain'! That's what the local welfare authorities called him, because they reckoned he was

always using his 'bad back' as an excuse for not going to work and claiming benefit instead. Actually, Vernon did stacks of different jobs to support his little family, including being a farm hand, a truck driver, a factory worker and a milk delivery man. He was also rumoured to be a moonshiner.

That meant he made and sold illegal whiskey (not that he polished orbiting satellites). Even though quite a few Elvis biographies say some unkind things about Vernon it's quite obvious that he really did care deeply about Elvis and Gladys. One of the most helpful (and profoundly thick) things Vernon ever said to Elvis was, 'I never met a guitar player worth a damn'. However, not long after this, he began a millionaire lifestyle all paid for by the efforts of his completely worthless guitar-playing son!

WELL, HE TURNED OUT TO BE MORE OF A SINGER THAN A GUITAR PLAYER!

Gladys Love Smith (1912–1958)

Gladys was Elvis's mum and loved him to pieces. She also came from a really poor family. Amongst other things she was famous for her delicious homemade gravy, biscuits and creamed potatoes, not to mention her all round niceness and homeliness. She also loved singing and dancing and was famous for her buck and wing (a dance, not a chicken dinner). After meeting at the local FAG (First Assembly of God) church in 1933, Gladys and Vernon had a whirlwind

romance and just eight weeks later they got hitched (hillbilly for married). Gladys was 21 and Vernon was 17 but pretended he was 22. In order to support the family while Vernon was otherwise unoccupied Gladys often had to go out to work. She toiled away in little clothes factories known as sweat shops.

Uncle Vester Presley (dates unknown)

Vester was Vernon's brother and helped him build his shotgun shack. He once said that listening to young Elvis singing made his teeth hurt. When Elvis got rich and famous he gave Uncle Vester the job of being gatekeeper at his mansion and a really swanky shirt to wear while he did it. Occasionally, Vester would be a bit slow at opening up for Elvis because he was asleep (or on some other planet  after drinking too much moonshine). So, not wanting to put his dear old uncle to any trouble, young Elvis would thoughtfully crash his car through the closed gates.

TERRIBLE TUPELO

After the death of Elvis's twin brother, Gladys was really worried that something bad would happen to Elvis himself so she was very, very protective towards him. Unfortunately, if you were as anxious about your little lad's wellbeing as Gladys was, East Tupelo wasn't really an ideal spot to bring him up.

At around that time it was more or less a shanty town, full of all sorts of nasties, including health threats like TB, rats the size of cats and cockroaches the size of rats, not to mention the terrible fires that broke out regularly amongst the wooden shacks. And just to make life *really* interesting, during the spring and early summer, the horribly destructive, rotating columns of air known as twisters, or tornadoes, would come roaring in and wreak havoc everywhere.

Whenever it looked like there was going to be a 'twister', Gladys would grab hold of little Elvis and high-tail it to the hills where they would hide in their hillbilly 'broom-cupboard' (cave) until the tornado had blown over.

The Tupelo Tornado

On 5 April 1936, when Elvis was just one and a bit years old, the mummy and daddy of all tornadoes devastated Tupelo. It only lasted five minutes but during that time it smashed 900 buildings to smithereens, caused masses of fires, killed more than 200 people and injured stacks more (not to mention blowing the feathers off chickens and the horns off cows). After it had gone, the Presleys' neighbours' homes and the local church across the road were all as flat as pancakes, but *amazingly* … Glad and Vern's little shack was *still* standing!!! Yes … OOOER!

Years later, Gladys said she reckoned that God (well known for his love of mind-blowing music) had deliberately spared Elvis from the twister because he was saving him up for a great future.

Gladys wasn't the only one who eventually decided that Elvis must have been 'chosen' for some sort of greatness. During a newspaper interview in the late 1950s, Vernon said that he'd realized there was something 'special' about his son when he'd seen a strange, dazzling blue light hovering near their little shack just around the time that Elvis was born (but then again, this wouldn't have been the first time Vernon had received a visit from the cops).

A piggy bank botch up

In 1937, when Elvis was just a tiddler, Vernon got a visit from the cops after he'd done something rather naughty. He'd sold a hog (a hillbilly pig) to his boss, Orville Bean, then changed the amount on the cheque Orville had given him for the porker. When Vern' and two pals dim-wittedly tried to cash the cheque they were caught and eventually sent to prison for three years.

Luckily Vernon was let out after only eight months but in the meantime Gladys was given a lean time by mean Mr Bean who chucked her and little Elvis out of the shotgun shack (the rotter!). They had to go and live with Gladys's cousin who later remembered how little Elvis used to sit on the porch crying because his dad wasn't there. Aah! Parchman Farm, the prison that Vernon was in, was miles away from Tupelo, so every time Gladys and Elvis wanted to visit him, they had to spend hours riding the local Greyhound bus through the Mississippi countryside.

When Vernon finally got out of prison he did all sorts of jobs – including building a prison! – but Vern and his little family still spent the next few years moving from one rented house to another and owing money right, left and centre. Whenever Elvis heard his mum and dad discussing all their financial problems it upset him no end so he told them they shouldn't worry because one day he'd make everything all right for them.

elvis's lost diary (Age 6-7)

September 1941

Today I been to school for my first time ever. Mama walked me to it so that no big boys was pickin' on me. But first she skrubbed my ears an face an neck real hard with her spechial sope what she makes herself. It is called East Tupelo Consolidated. My school not the sope. Mama said I must remember my manners wen I talk to the teachers an the groan ups. So I must say 'Yes sir! No sir!' and 'Yes marm! No marm!' all the time.

February 1942

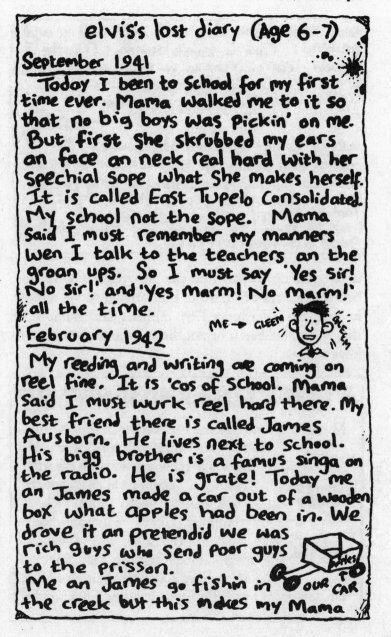

ME → CLEEN   CLEEN

My reeding and writing are coming on reel fine. It is 'cos of school. Mama said I must wurk reel hard there. My best friend there is called James Ausborn. He lives next to school. His bigg brother is a famus singa on the radio. He is grate! Today me an James made a car out of a wooden box what apples had been in. We drove it an pretendid we was rich guys who send poor guys to the prisson.

APPLES   OUR CAR

Me an James go fishin in the creek but this makes my Mama

21

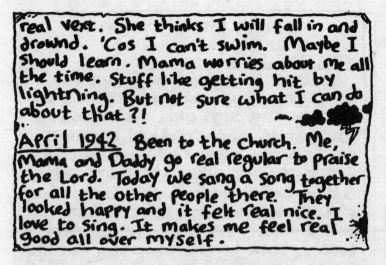

real vext. She thinks I will fall in and drownd. 'Cos I can't swim. Maybe I should learn. Mama worries about me all the time. Stuff like getting hit by lightning. But not sure what I can do about that?!

April 1942 Been to the church. Me, Mama and Daddy go real regular to praise the Lord. Today we sang a song together for all the other people there. They looked happy and it felt real nice. I love to sing. It makes me feel real good all over myself.

Elvis grew up to make people all over the world feel happy when they listened to him singing and as a result he was hero-worshipped by millions and millions of them! But, believe it or not, heroes themselves have to have heroes!

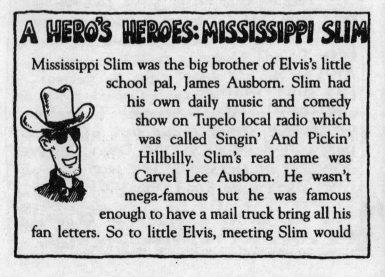

A HERO'S HEROES: MISSISSIPPI SLIM

Mississippi Slim was the big brother of Elvis's little school pal, James Ausborn. Slim had his own daily music and comedy show on Tupelo local radio which was called Singin' And Pickin' Hillbilly. Slim's real name was Carvel Lee Ausborn. He wasn't mega-famous but he was famous enough to have a mail truck bring all his fan letters. So to little Elvis, meeting Slim would have been like coming face to face with someone as famous as … er … Elvis Presley!

Elvis was always suggesting to James that they go see his brother at the radio station so he could get near to Slim who was a real 'laugh-a-minute' sort of bloke. (Yes, in addition to being a singing hillbilly, he was a blinking sillybilly.) Their visits to the studio gave Elvis his first taste of showbiz life and he was well impressed.

In 1944, when he was nine, Elvis actually got to sing on Slim's show with his hero backing him on guitar. Slim also taught Elvis some basic stuff about guitar playing, such as the finger positions for chords (and how it was much better to pluck it rather than blow it).

Little Elv' loved singing and was always humming and hollering the country and western tunes he heard on the radio and the gospel songs he heard in church. Well, he had to do *something* to keep his spirits up! He sang at home, he sang in church, and he sang in school. And he sang so *beautifully* that it gave his class teacher, Miss Grimes, an idea that brought him his first success.

COME AND ENJOY ALL THE FUN OF THE
MISSISSIPPI - ALABAMA
FAIR & DAIRY SHOW

TUPELO: TUESDAY 2nd – SATURDAY 6th OCTOBER 1945
You name it – We got it!
MULE-PULLING CONTEST! RODEO! CLOWNS!
PURTIEST ROOSTER COMPETITION! PURTIEST
MISS TUPELO COMPETITION! PURTIEST COW
COMPETITION!
WEDNESDAY 3RD – CHILDREN'S DAY
With a radio talent contest! Prizes donated
by 'WELO', your friendly local station. To be
held in the main grandstand (Seating for 2000!)

And don't forget - FAIRGRO...

THE FERRIS! THE OCTOPUS! ...WHIP
DODGEMS! HAUNTED HOUSE! ...
SHOOTING GALLERY! PEEPSHOWS!
FREAK SHOWS! AND MORE...

NOW THAT GIVES ME AN IDEA!

ELVIS'S LOST DIARY (AGE 10)

SEPTEMBER 15th 1945
Gettin' all excited! 'Cos the fair's comin'
to town real soon. Can't wait! It's just
the very best thing that happens here in
Tupelo. An' it lasts five whole days! Hmm.
I can already smell that sweet cotton
candy, an' them greasy dogs sizzlin' away
on hot griddles. And hear the
roar of them big machines what

24

drives the rides and the carny guys shouting for folks to come and see the shows. Got one itty bitty problem! It costs a whole lotta money to get in the fair. And I ain't got none! Figure I'm just gonna have to sneak in over the fence like last year... and the year before. I ain't gonna miss it for nuthin'. One day I'm gonna up an' run away an' join it! Then again, maybe not... it would hurt Mama and Daddy if I did! An no way am I gonna do that!

SEPTEMBER 28th

Yikes! I'm real antsy 'cos of somethin' Miss Grimes told me. She's entered me in the kids' singin' contest at the fair! 'Cos she thinks my singin's real ✹ pretty. I gotta stand up there in front of all them people 'n' holler away! Uh oh! Sure hope I'm up to it! Figure I'll do 'Old Shep' for my song. S'all about this dog saves a boy from drowning but then the dog gets worn out and the boy has to shoot him. Says somethin' like he wished they'd shot him instead of the dog. I done it before an' it near made them ol' teachers get all sad an'

SNIFF
BANG
OW!
BLUD

25

Sniffly. Hey! I just thought of somethin'! Being in the contest means I ain't gotta climb that pesky fence.

OCTOBER 3rd

This is a great day. 'Cos I've won a prize in the singin' contest. I stood up an' sung to that microphone an' thee was hundreds 'n' hundreds of people watchin' me an' when I finished they was all clappin' fit to bust! 'Specially Mama an' Daddy. They just about wore their hands off! Didn't get first prize though. Another kid from our school called Shirley Jones got that. But I won $5 and free goes on the Dodgems an' Whip an' everything for the whole day long. All that just for singin' a lil ol' Song! Maybe I'll do me some more of that!

A HERO'S HEROES: CAPTAIN MARVEL

When Elvis was little (and quite a bit bigger!) he collected and read superhero comics. His action strip faves were people like Batman, Superman, The Spirit and ... Plastic Man! (Don't say you've never heard of him!) But his all-time favourite was Captain Marvel, the caped conqueror who was forever flying into tricky situations and solving problems at the flick of a cartoonist's pen.

Elvis's childhood was full of difficulties that came from being poor but Elvis's unsuperhero-like dad wasn't that brilliant at solving them. So it would seem that the two-fisted, 'up and at 'em', over-achieving Captain Marvel was the fellow that little Elvis most wanted to be like, rather than the 'ooh me back's killing me, I'll just have me a rest for a couple of minutes' Vernon.

That may sound like utter twaddle until you know that a) when Elvis grew up he had Captain Marvel's lightning bolt and cape logo painted on the tail of his personal jet aeroplane; b) he had the same symbols engraved on the jewellery that he and his mates all wore; c) often, at the drop of a cheque book, he would change the lives of complete strangers who didn't have two dog biscuits to rub together by giving them money, cars and even houses; and d) in his later years Elvis loved wearing capes!

I SHALL NOW USE MY SUPER POWERS TO MAKE THIS HUGE PILE O' BURGERS DISAPPEAR!

ELVIS'S LOST DIARY (Age 11-13)

JANUARY 1946

I'm 11 today. I wanted a bicycle for my birthday but Mama said not. She was worryin' 'bout me as usual, thinkin' I'd get knocked off it or somethin'. So I've got a guitar. Which I don't think can hurt me none! But ain't so bad at all! Just gotta get me some lessons now. There was another tornado in Tupelo yesterday. Really spooked Mama an' me.

MARCH 1946

Been to the movies with Daddy. But we gotta keep it a secret. Our church, the First Assembly of God, don't like us visitin' the movie theatre. Nor dancin'! They say that if you watch a film, it's a sin! But gee! I love movies. They put me in another world. No bein' poor, no livin' in crummy places, no being pushed around... just nice houses and cars an' stuff. An' people laughin' an' singing. With pretty ladies havin' fun while handsome guys do heroic stuff. I'd give anything to be a movie star.

MAY 1946
Daddy let me drive our old
car again. I like doing
that.

OCTOBER 1947
   I been takin' my guitar to school some.
When it's recess an' lunchtimes us kids
sometimes go down in the basement. Me
an' a boy called Billy Welch do some
singin' and guitar playin' down there
while all the other kids gather round
an' listen. Makes me feel sorta
special!

OCTOBER 1948

At school the other day some rough kids
pinched my guitar. An' cut its strings!
Which made me cut up too! Dunno why
they did it? Maybe they hate my
music! But hey! Not long afterwards
some other kids bought me some new
strings for my guitar! Maybe them
ones like my music! I guess some folks
are just real bad and the others are
real good.   Mama told me we're leavin'
town real soon. Yes, again! (I've lost
count of the number of times we've moved
house.) She says we're flittin' 'cos
Daddy's got no job again. We're plain
broke. So tell me... What's new!

29

NOVEMBER 5th

I did a sorta leaving concert at school today. At the end this kid called Leroy came up to me and said, 'Elvis, one of these days you're gonna be <u>famous</u>!' So I said 'Sure hope so!' And yes, I really truly <u>surely</u> do! Can't do no more writin' 'cos Daddy's shoutin' for me to come an' load the old Plymouth with all our stuff.

NOVEMBER 6th

We quit Tupelo last night. Just like that! My old life and friends are gone! Now we're here in Memphis. This city's big, real big! It frightens me some. We're in our new apartment an' I hate it! We just got the one crummy room for everything... cookin', sleepin', livin'... the whole shootin' match! There's a bathroom down the passage but we're sharin' that with 16 other families! All their little kids mess it up somethin' terrible... so it STINKS! Seen a couple of rats too. Big as puppies! Shoot... whatta dump! Gonna look on the bright side though. Maybe movin' to this new town might make somethin' good happen...
                                    one day ?!

THE BEALE STREET BOOGIE

Lots of people reckon the Presleys' moonlight flit to Memphis in 1948 was the thing that changed thirteen-year-old Elvis's whole life! Why? Well, he had to walk a different way to school, didn't he? And go to a *different* school! His new one was called Humes High and he started it in September 1948. But more important than *that* ... Memphis was Music City *Tennessee*! Memphis was just *bursting* with all kinds of brilliant music!

Ever since the 1920s, Memphis had been home to tons of blues musicians, and when Elvis arrived great blues singers like B.B. King, Howlin' Wolf and Arthur 'Big Boy' Crudup were whippin' up a tornado of good sounds.

And as well as them there was the hillbilly music that Elvis got to hear on the local radio and the all night gospel singing sessions that took place just down the street from where he lived. Yes, Memphis was the perfect place to set his talent bubbling and simmering.

<u>1951</u> I dig Memphis so much. 'Specially Beale Street with all that great gospel and blues music what goes on. Not to mention all them cool cats chillin' out in their snappy threads. They buy 'em at a place called Lansky's. Gonna get me some too.

<u>AUGUST 1952</u>

Hmmph! Tried to get on the school football team but the coach threw me out on account of my long hair. Some guys just dont recognize style when they see it!

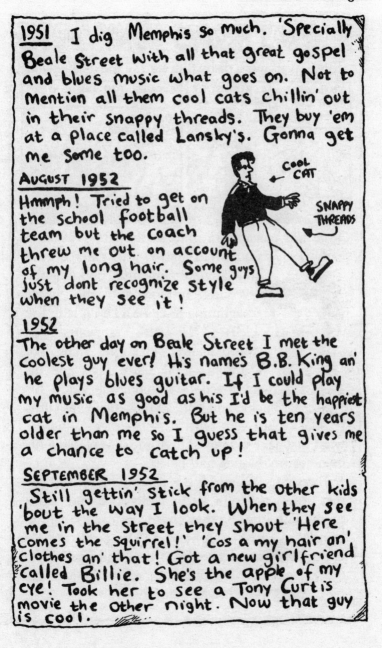

← COOL CAT

SNAPPY THREADS

<u>1952</u>

The other day on Beale Street I met the coolest guy ever! His name's B.B. King an' he plays blues guitar. If I could play my music as good as his I'd be the happiest cat in Memphis. But he is ten years older than me so I guess that gives me a chance to catch up!

<u>SEPTEMBER 1952</u>

Still gettin' stick from the other kids 'bout the way I look. When they see me in the street they shout 'Here comes the squirrel!' 'Cos a my hair an' clothes an' that! Got a new girlfriend called Billie. She's the apple of my eye! Took her to see a Tony Curtis movie the other night. Now that guy is cool.

A HERO'S HEROES: TONY CURTIS

Tony Curtis was a dishy film star … and a hair style!

I'D LIKE A TONY CURTIS, PLEASE

CERTAINLY, SIR. WON'T BE A JIFFY.

WOULD YOU LIKE HIM WRAPPED, SIR?

DIMWIT! I MEANT THE HAIRCUT!

Tone was megabig in films in the late 1940s and early 1950s and often played the parts of the newfangled 'juvenile delinquents' (young offenders) who were beginning to cause a kerfuffle in the USA. He also appeared in swashbuckling adventure films like *The Son Of Ali Baba*. Elvis and his mum loved to watch Tone swash his buckle and noticed how nicely his curly, jet-black hair went with his blue eyes. Which is what first gave blue-eyed Elvis the idea of dying his own browny-blonde hair black.

Years later, when Elvis was a big movie star, he met Tony on a film set in Hollywood and had a natter with him. As they chatted Elvis kept calling him 'Mr Curtis' so Tony said, 'Don't call me Mr Curtis. Call me Tony. What do I call you?' Elvis quickly replied, 'You can call me, Mr Presley!' Ha ha … Elvis was a laugh, wasn't he?

Taking care of hairpearances...

1 When Elvis was a teenager he used all sorts of stuff to make his hair darker. He's even said to have used shoe polish to achieve that special Tony tone.

2 Elvis wore his sideboards BIG! or 'truck-driver style', as he liked to call it. Well, he did drive a truck for a while! So there'd have been no point him wearing them 'brain-surgeon' style ... or Buddhist-monk style!

3 Once, when Elvis turned up to a new job, his new employer was gobsmacked by his hair and said he looked like: 'the original goon boy'! She was so disturbed by it that she actually sent him to her own (ladies) hairdresser to get it sorted!

4 Elvis sometimes used three sorts of hair oil. One for the back, one for the middle and...

Sorry about that ... and one for the *front*! They included vaseline, rose oil hair tonic and crewcut-duty 'butch' wax, which, despite sounding like something you'd smear all over a dog (or a sailor) is actually the stuff he put on his quiff so it would flop down in that oh-so-casual way while he was performing (but wouldn't actually fall off).

5 During the sixties and seventies Elvis's hair sometimes lost its lively, floppy look and occasionally resembled a large plastic helmet. After seeing him in a film, one unkind critic said his hair looked like...

6 When he got famous, Elvis's hair was insured for a million dollars. Quite sensible really. Somehow the idea of a completely bald Elvis wowing the fans seems highly unlikely...

I'M HAIR TO A FORTUNE!

Girls girls girls

What with his special-effects hair, perfect manners and striking good looks, Elvis became more and more and *more* popular with the girls. And of course, once he got to be famous, he had absolutely millions of them going crazy for him. Some people reckon that during his life he actually had *thousands* of girlfriends, especially if you include the ones who were his dates for just a short time. So naturally, in this lil ol' book, there's only going to be room for the occasional look at...

HIS LATEST FLAME: BILLIE WARDLAW

Billie was Elvis's neighbour in Memphis and she was one of his first ever girlfriends. Once, her and her mom saw him sitting outside in the dark singing and playing his guitar and Mrs Wardlaw told him he ought to be on the radio. So he told her that he *couldn't* sing (the modest *twit*). As well as being a great singer Billie reckoned that Elvis was a great kisser too. One day, when Elvis found a photo of another boy in Billie's wallet, he flipped his lid and started stamping on it because he was so jealous! And when she finally packed him in to go out with a sailor he cried his socks off.

The Sun Studios

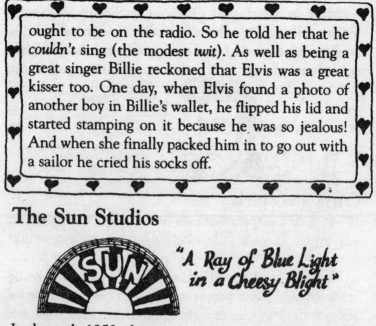

"A Ray of Blue Light in a Cheesy Blight"

In the early 1950s the main pop music charts in America were full of songs by the sort of musicians that *your* great grandparents may have listened to, like Frank Sinatra, Bing Crosby, Dean Martin, Doris Day and Perry Como. Their singing style was generally known as 'crooning' and they did it to a background of lots of slushy-sounding violins. Yes! It was the music that people now describe as easy listening. More like 'cheesy' listening?!

Apart from one singer called Johnny Ray who had a hit single called 'Cry', then followed his own advice by sobbing a lot on stage (no one ever found out what had upset him), there wasn't really anything to appeal to the newfangled teenagers who were dripping with dosh and bursting with energy but had no particular place to go (musically speaking that is).

GEE, I WISH SOMEBODY WOULD HURRY UP AND INVENT ROCK 'N' ROLL...

The only really hot 'n' happening music was being made by black musicians who'd been doing that sort of thing for a least the last 30 years but were more or less ignored by all of white America because in those days the USA was a *very* racist place!(Some of America's southern states were so racist that if an ambulance that was intended for white people happened to pass a badly injured black person, it wouldn't stop to pick them up!) In fact all of the brilliant R&B, gospel, blues and jazz discs that most white people were missing out on were actually called 'race' records because they were intended to be bought and listened to by black people *only*!

Sam Phillips was a white man who loved black music so much that he set up a recording studio in Memphis to record lots of great records. These included what is said to be the first rock and roll record ever: 'Rocket 88' by Jackie Brenston. Some of the best black musicians in America were more or less living on Sam Phillips' doorstep and as a result he made masses of brilliant discs. But tragically, because of all the racism, he could only sell them to black people! Sam knew deep down that if he could find a white singer who could sing in that brilliant black style he could make a million dollars. But what he *didn't* know was that the *very* person he was looking for was at that moment actually thinking about popping down to *his* studio!

ELVIS'S LOST DIARY (Age 18)

JUNE 3rd 1953

Left school today. Been down the employment office an' got me a job too! $33 a week at Parker's Machinists. Start tomorrow! Ooh ooh... big man now!

JULY 14th

Borrowed me $4 offa my boss to make me a vanity record[1] down at the Sun Studios. Just wanna hear myself on disc an' find out where I can get me some good payin' singin' gigs. An they'll be the people'll know.

JULY 15th

Been practisin' for doin' my record... Between you an' me, diary, what I really want is for them Sun people to hear me an' think I am great. Then ask

---

1. In those days home recording was almost unheard of so if you wanted to hear yourself on disc or tape (you vain thing!) you had to go to a studio and make a 'vanity' record.

me to be their recording artist. Perhaps I'm hopin' ~~ze~~ for too much? Maybe I'll tell 'em the record's for my mama's birthday... just to save me from bein' real embarrassed.

JULY 18TH

Been to the Sun Studios an' cut my record. I had a chat with the lady there. Well, she seemed kinda interested in my singin'... I think.

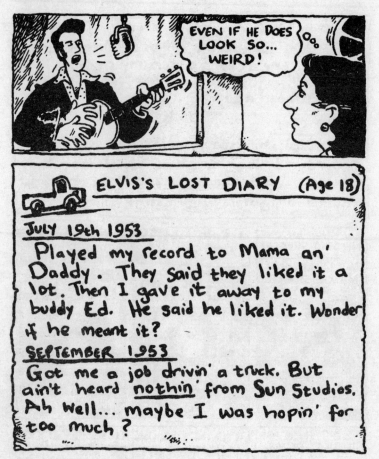

ELVIS'S LOST DIARY (Age 18)

JULY 19th 1953

Played my record to Mama an' Daddy. They said they liked it a lot. Then I gave it away to my buddy Ed. He said he liked it. Wonder if he meant it?

SEPTEMBER 1953

Got me a job drivin' a truck. But ain't heard <u>nothin'</u> from Sun Studios. Ah well... maybe I was hopin' for too much?

42

GO MAN... GO!

Elvis was desperate to hear from the Sun Studios. But they *didn't* call him! He sort of hung around outside a bit, popped in to make another vanity record and passed the rest of his time driving his truck, dating girls, getting a new 'steady' girlfriend called Dixie Locke, going to the movies and listening to his ever-growing record collection. Then, on the 26 June 1954, over a year after he'd made that first $4 'vanity' record, he got a phone call from the Sun Studios asking him to go down there to do some singing. He was off like a greyhound out of a trap. Years later, Marion, the studio manager, recalled how she'd only *just* put down the phone when he miraculously appeared at the studio, completely out of breath.

He did a bit of singing then Sam told him to come back for his first ever official recording session on 5 July … the day that would change Elvis's life for *ever*!

☼ ELVIS'S LOST DIARY (Age 19)

JULY 5TH 1954

Real hot today. 101 outside! Phew! Went along to Mr Phillips's studio for my first <u>real</u> recording session! Wore my best pink shirt, black pants with pink stripe down the side and the white shoes! Gotta look the business! First I did Harbor lights but Mr Phillips didn't seem too impressed. An' I was <u>a lot</u> nervous (which didn't help!). Then we had a Coke break an' while Mr Phillips was outta the room this song sorta popped into my head an' me an' Bill an' Scotty started goofing around with it. It was 'That's All Right Mama' which I learned offa Big Boy Crudup down on Beale Street. All of a sudden Mr Phillips stuck his head around the door an' yelled 'What's THAT!!?' And now he did look impressed. He said, 'Do it AGAIN!' So we did. And he had this BIG smile on his face.

<u>JULY 10th</u>

Oh man! I can't believe it! They're gonna play my record tonight! On <u>the</u> radio! Yeah, 'That's All Right Mama' by 'Elvis Presley' (me!) is gonna be heard by thousands of cats all around Memphis! But Elvis Presley ain't gonna be around for it! Because man, I'm just tooooooooooooo nervous! So I'm gonna go to the movies and lie low! But I've fixed the radio up to station WHBQ an' told Mama and Daddy to listen in for me.

<u>JULY 11th</u>

Man... is this really happenin'?! Last night I

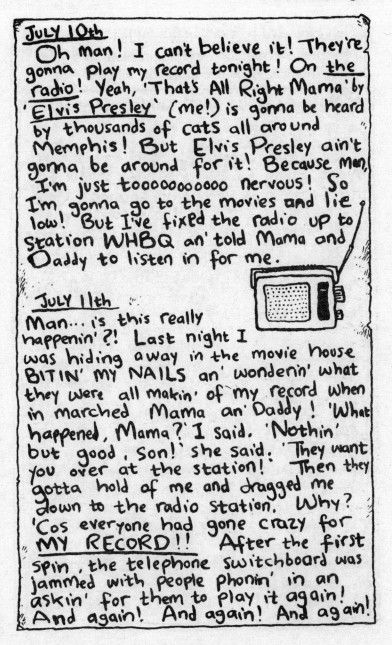

was hiding away in the movie house BITIN' MY NAILS an' wonderin' what they were all makin' of my record when in marched Mama an' Daddy! 'What happened, Mama?' I said. 'Nothin' but good, Son!' she said. 'They want you over at the station!' Then they gotta hold of me and dragged me down to the radio station. Why? 'Cos everyone had gone crazy for MY RECORD!! After the first spin, the telephone switchboard was jammed with people phonin' in an' askin' for them to play it again! And again! And again! And again!

So they did! Fourteen times! Back to back! When my folks finally got me to the studio I was shakin' all over! Dewey, the DJ, could see I was scared to death so he said we'd just chat while a record played and he'd let me know when he was ready to start the interview. He asked me stuff about my music an' what school I went to. After a bit I said, 'Ain't you gonna interview me yet?' an' he said, 'I just have! The mike's been open all the time!' An' man I broke out inna cold sweat! Thass right! He tricked me! But it was probably better that way!

July 20th

Shoot! This is all like a dream come true! My record's in the shops an' it's sellin' thousands! Girls are comin' up to me in the street askin' for my autograph!! (Wonder if Dixie's gonna be jealous?)

←ME

← GIRLS

Listen God! You know I'm a good boy who

loves his Mama and don't do wrong to no one, don't you? So please let this dream keep on happenin' to me God and please let me get real big and famous just like Mama said I would. An' then I'll be able to buy her an' Papa that mansion what I always promised them! And me a great big brand new CADILLAC!

Elvisology

- Eldene Beard was the first person <u>ever</u> to buy an Elvis record! At 9 a.m. on 19 July 1954 she walked into Charles Records on Main Street Memphis and bought 'That's All Right Mama' (and 15 pairs of earplugs).

- 'That's All Right Mama' is 1 minute 53 seconds long (or should that be short?). About one minute into it Elvis starts to sing nonsense. He didn't forget the words or anything. That's exactly what Arthur Crudup does in the original.

- Because of the racial prejudice that was about in southern states like Tennessee and Mississippi, black kids and white kids went to separate schools. Asking Elvis what school he went to was Dewey the DJ's crafty way of letting the radio audience know that Elvis was white. Elvis sang in a 'black' style but if the white listeners had thought for one moment that he was black it would have put them off buying his record. Pathetic, ain't it?

HIS LATEST FLAME: DIXIE LOCKE

Dixie was in Elvis's Bible study group at the local church and she said she could tell that God was really important to him from the way he prayed. (Maybe he wiggled while he worshipped?) They also met at the Memphis Rollerdrome. Elvis was wearing his bullfighter jacket, ruffly shirt and tight black pants with the pink stripe down the side and Dixie thought he looked really cool. They chatted, then went off in his car for burgers and milkshakes ... plus a little snog. They went out together for about  two years and were thinking of getting married but then Elvis began to get famous and while he was on tour getting even *more* famous he did a bit more snogging practice with lots of other girls. So Dixie married someone else ... and that was that!

Spreading the word

'That's All Right Mama' was definitely a big hit for Elvis. But it was *only* a hit in his local area. In a gi-normous country like America in the 1950s, with its thousands of local radio stations and record shops, and all its different record charts, it wasn't easy to become an instant nationwide success. So, even though he was fast becoming a big star in southern states like Tennessee,

Louisiana and Mississippi, Elvis was still more or less unheard of in far off places like…

But, as each day passed, more and more teenagers were telling their mates about the new singing sensation who was doing one night stands around Tennessee and the neighbouring states at sports stadiums, dance halls and 'sock hops' held in school gyms (where the dancers ditched their shoes and danced in bobby sox so they didn't damage the gym floor). And, of course, it wouldn't be long before the newspapers got to hear of the boy wonder who was knocking the bobby sox off almost every teenager in the south. All it needed now was a lil ol' rock 'n' roll riot!

JACKSONVILLE JOURNAL

May 14th 1955

BOY WITH RUBBER LEGS IN 'SOCK' AND ROLL RIOT!

Last night an almost unknown musician caused a full scale riot at the Gator Bowl here in lil ol' Jacksonville! Elvis Aaron Presley (20) from Memphis, Tennessee was at the root of the trouble. Local high school cheerleader, Billie Jo Pom Poms (17) told us. 'We'd heard of this Elvis but we'd never seen him. Oh man ... what a shock we got! What a singer! What a mover!! He was ...

GRRREAT! Look, this is his ... shirt button! Isn't it gorgeous!? You can have a feel if you like!'

However, Reverend Elijah Harshrasp (103) wasn't quite so keen on Elvis Presley.

When we asked him what he thought of young 'Wiggle Hips', the Revd leapt on a chair and yelled, 'The Devil has sent him to steal our children. Plug up their ears with quick-setting cement and lock them up, now!'

WHAT STARTED IT ALL?

Wayne Bob Greaseball (16) told us, 'By the time this amazing guy had finished his last song we were all going crazy! Yes! All 14,000 of us! As he left the stage he leaned into his microphone all sweaty and sneering and steaming and still wiggling a bit and just sort of breathed, 'Girls, I'll see *y'all* backstage!' And they believed him! Ten thousand screaming girls charged him and chased him back to his dressing room. Then they began ripping his clothes off! Gee I wish I was that Elvis Presley! Some guys get all the luck!'

Marshall Hank McNab said, 'When we finally got the riot under control we found him crouched on top of one of the shower stalls! His frilly pink shirt and jacket had been torn to shreds and he was covered in bruises and lipstick. And they'd even took his shoes and socks! They were like wild beasts!'

Vernon Presley (Elvis's dad) revealed, 'I thought they were going to kill him! And look what they did to his Cadillac!'

Editor's comment: Here at the Journal we get the feeling we ain't seen nothin' yet! Young Elvis Presley is going to be big, big, big!

A 'knee-jerk' reaction!

Ever since he'd been a nipper Elvis had had the nervous habit of jiggling his leg about. It was something he did to use up his surplus energy. So when he went on stage, the leg-wiggling happened quite naturally, often when he'd backed away from the microphone during the rest of the band's instrumentals. But the reaction it caused was *sensational*! Every time Elvis twitched his leg, the audience went crazy! At first he didn't seem to realize what was going on. He even thought that when they were all *hollerin'* (as he so quaintly put it) they were actually making fun of him! But his sharp-eyed manager soon spotted the phenomenal pulling power of a twitching, killer leg and he encouraged Elvis to 'shake that thing' all the more! Elvis soon got the idea! In his own words:

The more I did ... the wilder they went!

SCREEAM!

He soon developed lots of other subtle and charming ways of driving his adoring audiences into an uncontrollable frenzy. Like taking his wad of chewing gum out of his mouth part way through his act and lobbing it into the audience. This would instantaneously cause a mad scrap as everyone fought to get their hands on this tasteful Elvis '*chewvenir*'! Crazy, isn't it? (What they'd have done if he'd been in the habit of flicking the occasional stray bogey just doesn't bear thinking about!)

Rockabilly rebel

Elvis's music was a mixture of all the stuff he'd been listening to since he was knee-high to a boll-weevil ... blues, gospel, country and western and stacks of other stuff. But as with anything that's a bit new or different, quite a lot of people had no idea what to make of it!

This new music that Elvis and a few other musicians were playing eventually became known as Rockabilly. Elvis's manager gave Elvis the nickname of the Hillbilly Cat. Hillbilly for his country and western feel and cat for his cool cat, black music style. He didn't stay the Hillbilly Cat for long though. Quite soon the whole world would be calling him the King of Rock and Roll!

COLONEL TOM TAKES OVER

The word was out on Elvis Presley, the hot young hillbilly who made girls scream and boys grind their teeth with jealousy. Sooner or later a shrewd operator would hear of him and move in for a slice of his amazing action. For years Colonel Tom Parker had been dabbling in class acts like body-popping circus ponies and cha-cha-cha-ing chickens. He'd even been manager to a country and western singer (who'd sacked him) but now he was after something really BIG! The moment he saw Elvis he knew he'd found what he was looking for. A rocking and rolling chicken who would lay him gi-normous golden eggs for years to come!

BRILLIANT! ALL HE NEEDS IS EGGING ON!

After doing a deal with Sam Phillips in 1954, the Colonel took control of Elvis's career and set about organizing his astonishing, glittering, wealth-blessed future brilliantly. (He didn't do a bad job for Elvis either.) One of the first things he said to Elvis was...

Son, you have a million dollars worth of talent. By the time you're through you'll have a million dollars!

Young Elvis thought Tom was brill' and in 1957 he told a reporter...

The Colonel is more or less like a daddy when I'm away from my folks. Aaah! ... and Colonel Parker knows the business and I don't.

He was certainly right about that! The Colonel didn't just have *one* crafty scam up his sleeve ... he had a whole trick-shopful!

The making of Colonel Tom

The mysterious Colonel Tom might be either a) *Tom Parker*, the 'all American' orphan boy who was adopted by his Uncle Parker and later worked for him in the

Great Parker Pony Circus or b) Andreas Cornelius Van Kuijk, the 'all Dutch' teenager who came to America from Holland in 1929. Some people even say that 'Andreas' had had to flee Holland because he'd murdered someone! He was said to have entered America illegally without a passport and later changed his name to Tom Parker. In other words ... no one's quite worked out who Colonel Tom really was!

He was 'made' a Colonel by a country and western singer called Jimmy Davis (the one who wrote 'You Are My Sunshine'). This was his reward for helping Jimmy get to be the governor of Louisiana. He really liked the title and later on, when he was Elvis's manager and mega-rich and successful, he told everyone that they must always address him as 'Colonel'! (Rather than 'You Fat Conniving Two-faced Old Windbag!')

In the 1920s and 1930s there were hardly any tellies in America and people were fed up with traditional fun like cactus-hugging and bison-wrestling so they needed something else to keep them amused.

One of the big attractions was the enormous Royal American Carnival which consisted of 1,000 circus people and hundreds of circus animals who all travelled around America in a train ... 170 coaches long!

The Colonel worked for it and other travelling circuses and funfairs. He did all sorts: making the tea, telling fortunes, looking after the elephants, sticking up posters. At one time he had his own show which featured a monkey riding a pony in circles.

THIS ACT IS GOING NOWHERE!

The country folk who came to see this stylish and sophisticated performance paid their entrance with pop bottle tops which the Colonel later sold back to the drinks company. This was why the places the show visited were known as the Cherry Soda Circuit. Yes! The Colonel was in the pop business long before he met Elvis!

Tom was full of hokum and bunkum. Or to put it another way he was a confidence trickster. Here are five of his most famous scams:

• *The twelve inch hot dogs*. During the 1930s there was a fad for monster hot dogs. To cash in on the craze, Tom took an ordinary titchy little frankfurter sausage, cut it in two pieces and stuck them at either end of the twelve inch bun. He then filled the middle up with onions so that people wouldn't realize they'd been sold the hot dog with the 'less fattening centre'!

AND IT AIN'T EVEN MADE FROM A REAL DOG!

- *The 'day glo' canaries*. Crafty Tom caught sparrows and sprayed them with yellow paint then sold them as pets to bird brains who were daft enough to believe they were canaries!

- *The dancing chickens*. This one's cruel and fowl so you mustn't read it! Tom made chickens dance to the tune 'Turkey In The Straw' by making them leap around on an electrically heated cooking plate which he'd hidden ... under a load of straw!

- *The elephant dung bung*. Tom spread loads of elephant poo on the ground outside his circus tent. When people came 71 the performance they didn't want to walk in it so Tom made them pay for the privilege of riding his circus ponies across it!

- *The digitally enhanced quick-change trick*. The Colonel had a quarter-dollar piece welded to the ring on his little finger. With some nimble sleights of hand and distracting chatter he made people think they were getting the correct change when they bought tickets for shows but really he was diddling them out of

25 cents. Work it out! If he pulled this on 400 mugs a week that'd be a $100! It was said that of all the Colonel's crafty scams, this was Elvis's personal favourite. (Tut tut, naughty Elvis!)

In 1940, as a change from fairs and circuses, Tom became the official dog-catcher of the town of Tampa in Georgia. Being an imaginative and creative bloke, he decided to give the business a few personal touches. He dressed himself and Bevo Bevis (his personal assistant) in those long white laboratory coats that scientists wear. They were actually old dentist smocks (donated by some old dentists). They then tidied up the yard of the pooch prison and made a grave for a little doggy called Spot. Actually, Spot's spot was empty. Because Tom had invented him ... on the spot! However, failing to spot that Spot was not in the plot, people who'd lost their own pets asked if they could have similar little resting places created for their own dear departed Rovers and Tibbleses. Tom got Bevo to knock up little pet tombstones and coffins and in no time at all they had a thriving pet cemetery going. As solemn music played and the coffins were lowered into the ground Tom said prayers...

...then charged the owners $100 each for the service!

Colonel Tom was reported to have the ability to hypnotize people. It was said that this was what made him such a successful dog-catcher. Instead of chasing stray dogs around with an oversized butterfly net he would just look into their eyes and they'd immediately fall under his spell.

Apparently, he even put Elvis's bodyguards under his spell and ordered them to get down on all fours and bark and oink and moo and behave like farmyard animals (which, of course, came perfectly naturally to quite a lot of them). One day when Elvis was on a movie set Tom hypnotized his enormous bodyguard to go over to the director and tell him the film was a load of tripe. The director was so furious.

Some people claimed that Colonel Tom even hypnotized Elvis before he went on stage.

Five deeply dodgy tips on how to become a rock 'n' roll manager in the style of 'Colonel Tom Parker'

1 Keep a 'watch' on expenses!

One day when Elvis was filming a surfing scene the Colonel noticed that he was wearing his *own* watch on the movie set! He immediately blew his top and pointed out to the film company that they'd agreed to provide *all* of Elvis's outfits for the movie, including watches! He then told them that if they expected 'his boy' to go to the *time* ... and trouble of wearing his *own* watch for the movie it was going to cost them an extra ... *twenty-five thousand dollars*!

At another time the Colonel was negotiating with a promoter for a European concert-tour deal for Elvis and the promoter told him he'd pay one million dollars. With the dollar signs whirring in the spot where his eyeballs used to be, Tom replied, 'Well, that takes care of me. Now, how much you gonna give the boy?'!

2 Keep your boy in ignorance.

Whenever he could, Colonel Tom made sure Elvis didn't get to meet the people who wrote his music. Why? Because they were being paid peanuts for songs that were making him and Elvis mega-rich. Tom knew how generous Elvis could be and didn't want him feeling

61

sorry for the songwriters and suggesting they get a rise. Years later, Mort Shulman, who helped write *at least 16* of Elvis's greatest hits, said that even though Elvis gave Cadillacs to complete strangers he'd never even got so much as a Christmas card from him!

3 Realize that your merchandise is … priceless!
At one 1956 Elvis concert in Memphis someone asked Colonel Tom why there wasn't a price on the programmes. He told them that you should never put a price on anything and that way you could sell it for whatever people would pay. In Memphis, where people weren't so well off he charged a dime for the programmes but in Vegas where they were rolling in mazuma he made them pay two dollars for them.

4 Don't miss a trick to make dosh quick.
The Colonel used every opportunity to make money out of Elvis. When the Elvis concerts started to attract huge crowds he bought loads of spare binoculars from the American army and then rented them out to fans so they could be 'real close' to their hero.

Then, knowing they'd all be desperate to take Elvis home after the show, he sold them Elvis photos for two dollars each.

5 Have some nerve!

Richard Nixon, the President of America, wanted Elvis to give a concert at the White House so his helper rang Colonel Tom who said Elvis would consider it an honour and the fee would be $25,000! The helper was gobsmacked and said…

NO ONE GETS PAID FOR PLAYING FOR THE PRESIDENT!

WELL, I DON'T KNOW ABOUT THAT, SON, BUT THERE'S ONE THING I DO KNOW. NOBODY ASKS ELVIS PRESLEY TO PLAY FOR FREE!!

So, with a talent the size of Texas and a 'got every angle covered' manager like Colonel Tom, Elvis was all set to hit the big time! Which is *exactly* what he did.

ATOMIC ELVIS

Look back over the past 12 months of your life. You're probably really proud of some of the stuff you've achieved. You know the sort of thing ... grown two inches taller, learned to spell ~~seperate~~ separate, taught yourself to play the Mongolian nose flute whilst plucking your teeth. Yeah ... well, sorry to disappoint you, but next to what Elvis did in 1956, that is ... *nothing*!

1956 was Elvis's astonishing year. The year he went atomic, ballistic, rocket-propelled *and* supersonic, <u>all</u> in one!

On 1 January 1956, Elvis was an averagely well-known 20-year-old rock 'n' roller. Only 12 months later he was a world-famous, millionaire megastar, earning more than any other entertainer in America. And he was still only 21!

At the beginning of the year hardly anyone twigged that Elvis was about to become such a galloping, gobsmacking, 'overnight' success. One stingy newspaper gave a photographer the job of following Elvis around and taking snaps of him but told him that the young rock 'n' roll hillbilly from Tennessee just wasn't worth using colour film on.

The 3,800 black and white pictures that photographer took are now some of the most admired and famous images of Elvis ever.

Even the big bosses of Elvis's new record company were really worried that taking him on might lose them loads of money. They couldn't have been more wrong! By the end of March 1956 he'd become their best-selling performer and eventually ended up selling more records than *all* of their other artists put together! They were having so much trouble keeping Elvis-crazy fans supplied with his music that they had to ask other record companies if they could borrow their machinery to help them produce enough discs to meet the huge demand. And by December they'd sold more than *ten million* of his records.

NO! I SAID BORROW ANOTHER RECORD PRESS!

THE PANTS-B-TIDY TROUSER PRESS

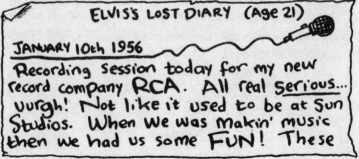

ELVIS'S LOST DIARY (Age 21)

JANUARY 10th 1956

Recording session today for my new record company RCA. All real serious... uurgh! Not like it used to be at Sun Studios. When we was makin' music then we had us some FUN! These big business guys seem more interested in money, money, money... rather than whippin' up a good-times tornado! One of the numbers we did was called 'Heartbreak Hotel'. The guys who wrote it got the idea when they read about a suicide note from someone who said that he 'walked a lonely street'. Poor guy! It's real weird and gloomy... but a great song. We done it with tons of echo an' it sounds real cool! My record company aren't so sure about it though. Well, we'll see... won't we!

JANUARY 25th

Met the big boss man of RCA today. When we shook hands I got him with my trick buzzer... ha ha ha! I'd hidden it in my palm. You shoulda seen his face! Mr Sholes, my record producer, didn't seem too impressed though. He looked like he wanted the ground to swallow him up or something. Wonder why?

JANUARY 27th

'Heartbreak Hotel' released today. Got all my fingers crossed!

FEBRUARY 1ST

Hey! I just been on TV...
for the second time ever. An'
boy, when I walked out in front of
them TV cameras, was I nervous!
So I started up with Big Joe Turner's
'Shake, Rattle and Roll'. Ha ha!
Mr Parker says TV's the way to go!
More 'n' more people are getting 'em an'
he reckons we can reach more fans through
through just one show than in a
lifetime of concerts. I'd never
thought a that! He's a smart
guy, Mr Parker! Anyway, by the time
I finished my act I felt great!
Going on tour now.

FEBRUARY 4th

Came back off tour to do another TV
show! I did 'Baby Let's Play House' and
'Tutti Frutti'. Straight back on tour
again tomorrow! Lawdy... Lawdy!

FEBRUARY 21ST

We been touring the East Coast and
Florida. And working most every single
day. Boy, I'm pooped! We pull into
some town, go to the hotel room, get
washed up. An' sometimes we go straight
to the concert hall or movie house to
do our show. Then after that it's
straight back in our cars an' we start

driving to the next town. All we do is drive-play-drive-play-drive! But I love it! An' I love my fans. The louder they scream the harder I work! I just wanna give them everything!

FEBRUARY 23rd

Yikes! I been in the cotton pickin' hospital! We was just loadin' up the instruments after a concert when I went out cold! The doctor reckons I been overdoing it with all these live shows! He told me I was doin' more work in 20 minutes wigglin' an' singin' than a labourin' guy does in a whole 8 hours! Told me to rest up. Fat chance! Them pretty itty-bitty nurses just wouldn't leave me alone! Not that I care! Anyway, I checked out of the hospital and did my concert at the Gator Bowl like I was s'posed to. I can't let my fans down, can I? Love 'em to pieces!

Elvis's fans really were one of the most amazing things about 1956. They seemed to appear from nowhere. It seemed like one day there were just a few thousand and the next there were absolutely *millions*. They were all over the place ... following him around, besieging his mum and dad's house, trying to climb in his bedroom window *and* going completely crazy at his concerts! And it wasn't just his records they bought by the factoryful. They made him and Colonel Parker very happy (and very *rich*) by spending 26 million dollars (that would be approximately a mere $160 million nowadays) on Elvis souvenirs during just six months in 1956! Yes, even *more* than they spent on his records.

Now you know what they looked like! Here's some of the *very* weird stuff they did!

Presley-maniacs...

1 Sometimes look ... for-lawn!

Elvis used some of his mega-bucks to buy his mum and dad a nice new house with an open-plan garden. After a while they had a big fence put round it because fans were forever coming in and nicking stuff. One fan phoned the Presleys' next door neighbour and said she just *had* to have some grass from Elvis's garden and would they send her some. The neighbour's son said that it would be much easier to send some grass out of their own garden but his mum insisted that it had to be genuine Elvis grass. It was a real turf challenge but the young blade nipped next door and got a bit of grass which they then sent to the girl. The girl was so chuffed that she wrote a thank you note saying 'That grass changed my life!'

2 Are dust nuts!

A movie director called Hal Kantner who was going to direct and write one of Elvis's films couldn't quite get his head round just how amazingly popular Elvis had become, so he decided personally to check him out at one of his concerts. When he arrived, a mob of fans mistook his big posh car for Elvis's and came crowding around it. He noticed one of the girls open her handbag and take out a paper tissue. He was then astonished to see her wiping his car with her hand and carefully putting the dust she'd collected into the paper tissue. She then folded the tissue, put it back in her bag and scampered off looking as if she'd just been given the keys to Elvis's toy cupboard.

3 Have the screaming abdabs ... without knowing it!

When Elvis was starting out and doing local gigs his manager used to pay a couple of girls to do a bit of screaming so that the rest of the audience would get the general idea of how to react to young swivel-hips. Screaming is contagious (like flu ... and yawning). After a while the audiences just went into scream mode automatically so the rentagobs lost their jobs. All it took was for Elvis to walk on stage, curl his lip (Elvis curled his lip like other people curl their hair), pluck his guitar a couple of times and the whole audience would be screeching louder than a flock of seagulls who've just found a three-day-old fish supper on a rubbish heap. One fan reported being astonished at hearing an amazing wailing sound coming from the audience at one concert and then being *even more* astonished when they suddenly realized that they were making it too. And that was a boy! (Maybe he was screaming with *fear* at being surrounded by thousands of screaming girls?)

By the spring of 1956 the fans were screaming so loudly that Elvis's backing band had no idea what he was singing. They had to watch his body movements for clues as to what and how they were supposed to be playing. One of Elvis's backing musicians once said that it was like being in a 'sea of sound' and that they were the only band in history to be directed by a bottom!

4 Are sofa'natical.
After one concert Elvis stayed the night at a friend's house and slept on their sofa. The next morning a fan spotted Elvis driving away from the house. Not long afterwards the girl and about ten billion of her crazed mates charged into the house without so much as an 'Excuse me we believe Elvis Presley slept here last

night … do you mind if we come in and soak up some of the unique atmosphere that surrounds the great man?'

As soon as the fans ran into the sitting room they spotted the crumpled sheets on the sofa and realized that must have been where Elvis had kipped. They pounced on the poor defenceless piece of furniture and began knocking the stuffing out of it. Just moments later all that was left of it was its wooden frame

5 Are hairo worshippers.

A radio DJ told his listeners that he'd got seven strands of Elvis's hair to give away. Yes, *seven*. He said that the hairs were genuine and that he had a signed witness statement to prove it. 5,000 fans rang to demand a strand!

6 Are head-bangers and sweat-hearts!

As Elvis was performing at a gig in San Antonio in Texas, fans fell on to their knees and beat their heads on the floor as he sang.

Elvis perspired quite a lot when he performed. After the concert some fans discovered a huge lagoon of sweat that had actually dribbled, dripped and squirted from the glands of the great rock 'n' roller himself. (Well, it was a bit of a damp patch actually.) They immediately got down on the floor of the stage and began rolling around in the stuff.

7 Are avid letter-writers.

By 1956 Elvis's fan club was receiving 4,000 letters every day (and, of course, Elvis carefully read each one and replied to it personally). When a British journalist said that Elvis's film, *Jailhouse Rock*, was just a load of bad taste and violence and that Elvis was a bore, the fans wrote *him* lots of letters too! Not love letters ... but hate mail. The bad-mouthing newspaperman received so many poison-pen letters that the paper printed a whole page of them alongside a picture of him being hanged! (But non-violently ... and all in the best possible taste, of course!)

8 Are easily foiled.

When Elvis stayed at hotels he had the windows of his room covered with silver foil so that he could pretend day was night and get some much-needed rest. The moment he left one motel the manager took the foil down and cut it into one inch squares which he then sold to Elvis fans for a small fortune.

9 Are easily pleased.
When Elvis came home to Memphis once and was being mobbed by fans, one of them grabbed his hand (ooer!) so he just grinned and said,

So she did and a tense and thrilling hand-grasping situation was over in just seconds. Later on, whilst describing her incredibly dramatic and life-altering '*letting go of Elvis's hand*' experience to reporters, the girl said: 'It was heavenly!' Thank goodness he didn't ask her to *marry* him! She's probably still telling that story to her grandchildren.

10 Regularly get carried away.
When the fans got completely carried away and rushed towards the stage in a desperate attempt to touch Elvis,

snog him, steal his trousers, tell him they loved him, etc. they were usually intercepted by his minders. And then they got carried away all over again! Ha!

At one concert in Kansas City a huge herd of rabid fans decided to charge him all at once so the security men were unable to stop them. In no time at all the stage was overrun by steaming teenagers and during the chaos that followed they threw Elvis's drummer, DJ Fontana, into the orchestra pit (the hole where the big band usually sit).

Elvis didn't seem to mind any of this wild behaviour one bit. When he was asked what he thought about them he said…

The fans are my life-blood – without them I'd be nowhere.

AND I'D STILL BE UP ON THAT STAGE…

Elvis! On my forecourt! Well I'll be … darned!
The more fans Elvis got, the more difficult it became for him to do ordinary everyday things, like getting his car checked over…

78

THE PETROL STATION MANAGER GOT REALLY UPSET BY ALL THE BODS MILLING ROUND HIS FORECOURT...

HEY BUDDY... MOVE YA CAR! YOU'RE BLOCKIN' UP MY BUSINESS! SO SCRAM!

I CAN'T – I'M TRAPPED.

THE MANAGER WASN'T THE PATIENT SORT...

MAYBE THIS'LL SPEED YOU UP!

BOOO!

WAP

OW!

ELVIS DIDN'T TAKE THAT SORT OF THING SITTING DOWN...

DON'T GET PHYSICAL WITH ME, PAL!

DOOOSH!

URRRGHDFFF!

HURRAW!

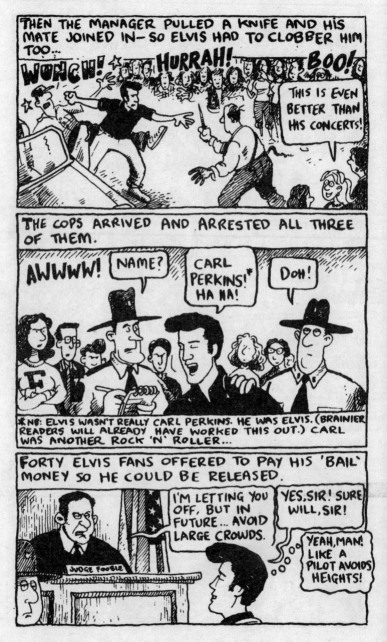

THEN THE MANAGER PULLED A KNIFE AND HIS MATE JOINED IN— SO ELVIS HAD TO CLOBBER HIM TOO...

WUNCH! ☆ HURRAH! BOO!

THIS IS EVEN BETTER THAN HIS CONCERTS!

THE COPS ARRIVED AND ARRESTED ALL THREE OF THEM.

AWWWW! NAME? CARL PERKINS!* HA HA! DOH!

*NB: ELVIS WASN'T REALLY CARL PERKINS. HE WAS ELVIS. (BRAINIER READERS WILL ALREADY HAVE WORKED THIS OUT.) CARL WAS ANOTHER ROCK 'N' ROLLER...

FORTY ELVIS FANS OFFERED TO PAY HIS 'BAIL' MONEY SO HE COULD BE RELEASED.

I'M LETTING YOU OFF, BUT IN FUTURE... AVOID LARGE CROWDS.

YES, SIR! SURE WILL, SIR!

YEAH, MAN! LIKE A PILOT AVOIDS HEIGHTS!

JUDGE FOOBLE

JET-PROPELLED PRESLEY

By the spring of 1956, Elvis's life was getting just a little bit hectic. Why? Because it seemed like almost everybody in America wanted a piece of the Presley action. His recording company had at long last realized they'd got a one-man money-making machine on their hands so they wanted him to cut more and more discs. He was booked to do a whole load of TV shows from New York. Just about every concert hall in America wanted him for live appearances. And he still had to perform on the radio shows that he'd begun doing when he first got famous.

And, as if all that wasn't enough, Colonel Parker cranked up the Presleymania to exploding point by getting the Hollywood movie moguls interested in 'his boy'. In other words Elvis needed to be in *thousands* of places at the same! But, without cloning him, this was impossible. So he did the next best thing and jetted backwards and forwards across America.

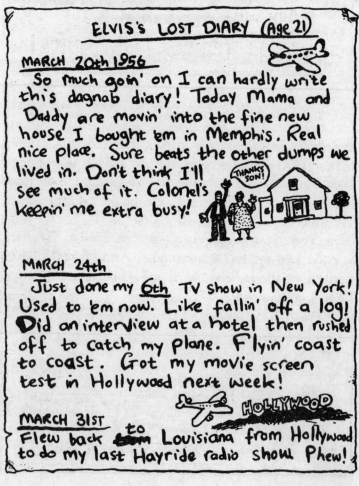

ELVIS'S LOST DIARY (Age 21)

MARCH 20th 1956

So much goin' on I can hardly write this dagnab diary! Today Mama and Daddy are movin' into the fine new house I bought 'em in Memphis. Real nice place. Sure beats the other dumps we lived in. Don't think I'll see much of it. Colonel's keepin' me extra busy!

THANKS SON!

MARCH 24th

Just done my **6th** TV show in New York! Used to 'em now. Like fallin' off a log! Did an interview at a hotel then rushed off to catch my plane. Flyin' coast to coast. Got my movie screen test in Hollywood next week!

HOLLYWOOD

MARCH 31ST

Flew back to Louisiana from Hollywood to do my last Hayride radio show. Phew!

APRIL 1ST

Flew back to Hollywood from Louisiana for my screen test with Mr Hal Wallis, the bigshot movie director. They got me to sing to one of my own records while I pretended to play a stringless guitar. But no way do I just wanna be a guy who sings in movies! Wanna be a ~~proper~~ movie star... like Brando an' Jimmy Dean an' Rod Steiger! Don't even wanna sing in 'em at all! Just do actin'... Off to San Diego for another TV special.

APRIL 3rd

Did my TV show from an aircraft-carrier deck with Miltie Berle. He's Mama's favourite comic. I did 'Blue Suede Shoes' an' afterwards he came out wearing giant blue suede shoes an' pretendin' to be my twin brother Melvin! Ha ha...(Hey, hope the twin bit didn't upset Mama!)

ME → ← MILTIE

A REAL BIG AIRCRAFT ~~CAREER~~ CARRIER

SOMEDAY APRIL THE SOMETHING OR OTHER!!? ← (Have lost all track of time!)

Had problems at my San Diego Arena show last night. The fans went crazy an' did another lil' ol' riot for me. Couldn't even hear myself sing! So I just stopped right there an' said, 'Sit down or the show ends!' And they did. Felt just like a big ol' school teach'. With <u>thousands</u> of kids in my class.

APRIL 6th

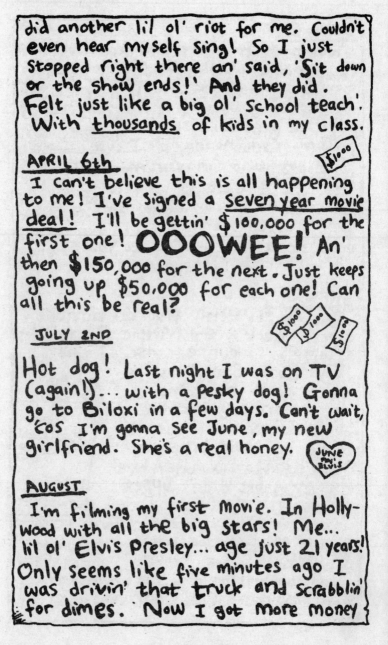

I can't believe this is all happening to me! I've signed a <u>seven year movie deal!</u> I'll be gettin' $100,000 for the first one! **OOOWEE!** An' then $150,000 for the next. Just keeps going up $50,000 for each one! Can all this be real?

JULY 2ND

Hot dog! Last night I was on TV (again!)... with a pesky dog! Gonna go to Biloxi in a few days. Can't wait, 'cos I'm gonna see June, my new girlfriend. She's a real honey.

AUGUST

I'm filming my first movie. In Hollywood with all the big stars! Me... lil ol' Elvis Presley... age just 21 years! Only seems like five minutes ago I was drivin' that truck and scrabblin' for dimes. Now I got more money

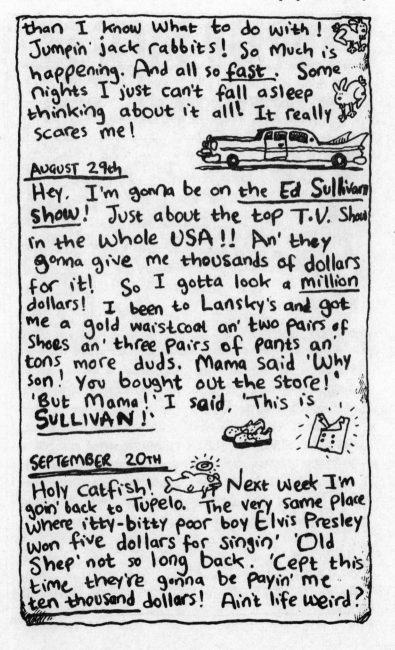

than I know what to do with! Jumpin' jack rabbits! So much is happening. And all so _fast_. Some nights I just can't fall asleep thinking about it all! It really scares me!

AUGUST 29th

Hey. I'm gonna be on the Ed Sullivan show! Just about the top T.V. show in the whole USA!! An' they gonna give me thousands of dollars for it! So I gotta look a million dollars! I been to Lansky's and got me a gold waistcoat an' two pairs of shoes an' three pairs of pants an' tons more duds. Mama said 'Why son! You bought out the store!' 'But Mama!' I said, 'This is SULLIVAN!'

SEPTEMBER 20TH

Holy catfish! Next week I'm goin' back to Tupelo. The very same place where itty-bitty poor boy Elvis Presley won five dollars for singin' 'Old Shep' not so long back. 'Cept this time they're gonna be payin' me ten thousand dollars! Ain't life weird?

TUPELO TATTLER

SEPTEMBER 27th 1956

WELCOME HOME ... SON!

Yesterday was probably the proudest day in the history of lil ol' Tupelo because our boy ... came home! Yep, yesterday we had us an ELVIS PRESLEY DAY! The lil ol' poor boy who left this town just a few short years ago with holes in his lil ol' socks has returned. And we was ready for him with a real Tupelo-style wang-dang-doodle! We had us an Elvis Presley Day parade an' every shopkeeper in town decorated their window with an Elvis Presley theme.

Then our boy, Elvis Presley himself, appeared in person at the Alabama-Mississippi Dairy Show. Yup, the very same place where just eleven short years ago itty-bitty Elvis won his $5 for singin' 'Ol' Shep'. TV companies, movie newsreel guys, plus 50,000 (!!) cotton pickin' visitors came to town to see our boy do his thang! When Elvis got up on that there stage yesterday the mayor presented him with the key to the city (guitar-shaped of course!) and then our boy said that most times before when he came to the show he'd had to sneak over the fence to get in 'cos he didn't have no money and now we was payin' him to come here! How we all laughed. Ain't lil ol' life peculiar!

Well, when our boy started to strut his stuff on that there outdoor stage 20,000 itty-bitty Elvis fans started screamin' fit to bust and our local cops had to be helped by the National Guard to keep 'em off our boy! But that didn't stop one lil ol' fan rippin' the buttons off Elvis's blue velvet shirt what his mama had made him!

An' talkin' of our girl Gladys ... bein' the modest lil ol' thing she is she said it made her feel right bad comin' back to Tupelo where they had been so poor what with them bein' so stinkin' rich now! Oh shucks! Ain't she a sweetie pie! As for Vernon he just looked right proud! An' guess what that lil boy of theirs done gone and done with his $10,000 appearance money. Only gave it back so we could build a lil ol' Elvis Presley Youth Centre for the poor kids here! Says we should build them kids a lil ol' guitar-shaped swimmin' pool..

A right carve up! By the end of 1956 Elvis wasn't just *America*-famous ... he was *World*-famous! Teenagers everywhere had heard of him and were nuts about him. It seemed that the only person in the whole world who hadn't heard of him was ... a school teacher in England.

(But are you *surprised?*) When Elvis died in the 1970s a woman wrote a letter to *The Times* newspaper saying that the year Elvis went rocket-powered she'd just started her first teaching job and that one morning an elderly school mistress had walked into the staffroom in a right strop and said...

> *I must speak to a boy called Elvis Presley because he has carved his name on every desk in the school!*

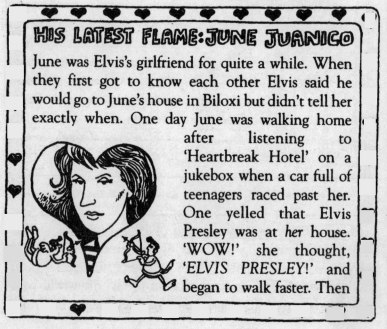

HIS LATEST FLAME: JUNE JUANICO

June was Elvis's girlfriend for quite a while. When they first got to know each other Elvis said he would go to June's house in Biloxi but didn't tell her exactly when. One day June was walking home after listening to 'Heartbreak Hotel' on a jukebox when a car full of teenagers raced past her. One yelled that Elvis Presley was at *her* house. 'WOW!' she thought, 'ELVIS PRESLEY!' and began to walk faster. Then she remembered that Elvis was *her* boyfriend ... so she started to run!

When she turned the corner into her street it was chock-a-block with people wanting to see Elvis. She fought her way through and found her mum in a right old tizzy. She told June that Elvis was really angry about the crowds so he'd gone off to Florida for some peace and quiet. June was devastated!

A bit later on, when they finally managed to get together again Elvis asked her why she'd told everyone he was coming to Biloxi and she said she hadn't but she joked that she *had* put up stacks of posters saying 'Elvis is coming! Elvis is coming!'. Elvis laughed and then they both felt loads better and had a snog.

Perhaps June should have pointed out that if you're a famous rock and roller and want to go unnoticed it's not a good idea to cruise into town in a giant white limousine with Tennessee number plates!

THE COLONEL SAID IF WE DON'T WANT THE FANS BOTHERING US WE GOTTA ARRIVE INCOGNITO...

NO CHANCE OF THAT- I CAN'T EVEN FIND COGNITO ON THE MAP!

Some staggering Elvististics

- During 1956, Elvis spent 26 weeks at number one in the charts and sold 12.5 million singles and almost three million albums in America alone.
- On 29 December he made chart history by having ten songs in the Top 100 at the same time.
- For the first half of the year, his record sales made up half of RCA's total income.

- 'Don't Be Cruel', which came out in July 1956, sold six million copies.
- 'Heartbreak Hotel', Elvis's first single for a big record company sold nearly a third of a million copies in just three weeks. It went on to sell thirty-eight million copies in its first five years of release.
- In his first ten years with RCA, Elvis clocked up over 115 million record sales.

The Colonel said to Elvis, 'Do as I say and your dreams will come true.' The Colonel *was* right! Now that the money was pouring in Elvis could make his wildest dreams come true. Like owning a fleet of...

The most fintastic cars in the world!

At the end of WW2 an automobile designer looked at the snazzy rear end of a Lockheed Lightning fighter plane and thought…

ACE FINS! WOULDN'T MIND CRUISING DOWN THE HIGH STREET WITH A COUPLE OF THOSE ON MY REAR!

So the designer dreamed up a *car* with tail fins. It was called a Cadillac and not only did the cool new cars have jet-fighter-style fins but they also had little bullety shaped bumps on their bumpers that looked just like the feisty little plane's nose. Soon the fins began to grow bigger and sharper and by the 1950s the 'fin wars' had begun, with car manufacturers all trying to outfin each other!

THOSE FINS ARE JUST TOO BIG!

But when it came to the coolest car of the decade, the Cadillac was still the fish's flippers. Just the car for a jet-propelled megastar to spend his new-found fortune on!

Our star and his cars

Here are some amazing facts about Elvis's driving ambitions!

• Elvis's first-ever Cadillac was painted pink and black to match his clothes. Vernon had a matching pink and black trailer made with Elvis's name written on the side for Elvis and the boys to cart their instruments around in (and to remind them who they were). One of Elvis's pals said...

It looked like a mobile toilet but Vernon acted like it was a luxury yacht!

- Elvis's most famous Cadillac was his super-duper gold one. It had gold-plated hubcaps, an in-car gold electric razor, two record players, a TV set and an electric shoe buffer. It was said to be painted with 40 coats of paint including diamond dust, real flakes of gold and gold fish scales (to match those *fins* of course!). So, if Elvis happened to park next to you and accidentally grazed your paintwork the value of *your* car would probably go up by at least $1,000!

- During the last ten years of his life Elvis owned at least 100 mega-expensive cars including Cadillacs, Rolls Royces and Ferraris. He usually had between eight and 15 at a time (so he didn't even have to leave his own front drive to get stuck in a traffic jam).

- Elvis learned to drive when he was ten and when he was 12 Vernon let him tootle around town in the family car. However, the old banger wasn't up to much and had a piece of cardboard in place of one of the windows.

HEY POP! SINCE YOU REPLACED THE WINDSHIELD WITH THIS CARD I ALWAYS SEEM TO BE CRASHING...

- Vernon bought Elvis his first car when he was a teenager but he'd only had it three months when it caught fire on the way to a show. Elvis and the band piled out with their stage clothes and instruments, then sat and watched it burn. Years later Elvis said that the horn had made a noise like a dying cow. He said he thought he was watching his whole career go up in smoke because the band relied on the car and often travelled 400 miles each day to get to and from their gigs.

- Between hitting the big time in 1956 and his death in 1977 Elvis bought at least 1,000 cars to give away to bodyguards, helpers, family and friends. Once, while doing a story about Elvis's generosity with cars, a TV reporter joked that if Elvis was watching, he'd sure like a nice new car too. Elvis *was* watching ... so he sent one!

- Elvis used to buy Cadillacs like other people buy toilet rolls. He once bought 13 in one go (Cadillacs, not toilet rolls). Actually, in the end, it turned out to be more than that! Here's why:

I'M GONNA GET ME IN THE MOVIES

As well as being music mad ... Elvis was *movie* mad. He had been ever since Vernon had defied their stuffy old church and snuck him in to see that first movie back in the 1940s. And when Elvis moved to Memphis he became even more of a flick fan because he got a part-time job working at a movie theatre. Which was great! He got paid for watching the films and a nice uniform to wear while he did it. (He *loved* uniforms and dressing up!) And now, one of his *other* wildest dreams came true, because good ol' Colonel Tom had gotten him the chance to be *in* the movies. At last, he could dress up to the nines *and* make out just like his favemost movie star ever!

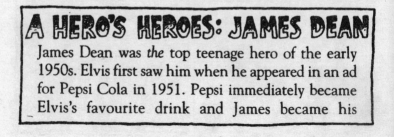

A HERO'S HEROES: JAMES DEAN

James Dean was *the* top teenage hero of the early 1950s. Elvis first saw him when he appeared in an ad for Pepsi Cola in 1951. Pepsi immediately became Elvis's favourite drink and James became his number one movie hero! James didn't actually sing or play the guitar like some of Elvis's other heroes did. He was just brilliant at sneering and mumbling, and looking mean, moody and magnificent! His stylish sneering and super-cool surliness caught the mood of America's 1950s teenagers perfectly. He was their rajah of rebelliousness and their czar of strop. Actually they didn't have *that* much to be bad-tempered or rebellious about because lots of them were having a great time! But that isn't the point, is it? When you're a teenager you just have to make a fuss about *something*! In 1955 James made a brilliant movie called *Rebel Without A Cause*, in which he played a teenage tearaway who shouts at his parents a lot and drives cars at cliff edges to prove to the local toughs that he isn't a chicken.

Just two weeks before *Rebel Without A Cause* was released, James was killed in car crash. Some people said that he crashed his mega-trendy sports car because he wasn't wearing his mega-untrendy specs. (Yup! Typical rebel.) Despite him being dead, fan letters continued to pour in at 2,000 a week … for the next three years! The wreckage of his car was put on exhibition in Los Angeles. 800,000 fans (or ghouls, as some might say) paid to gawp at the mangled metal. And if they paid a bit extra they got the *really* big thrill of sitting in the driving seat that James had died in! People reckon that shuffling off his sneakers at 24 was a really neat career move for James, because now everyone remembers him as a tragic young star instead of a wrinkly has-been.

Rebel Without A Cause, or 'Rebel Without A Pebble'! as Elvis called it, was Elvis's favouritest film ever. He knew the whole script off by heart. He should have done! He watched it more than a hundred times!

People predicted that Elvis would be the James Dean of Rock 'n' Roll but after his hero died Elvis spotted a brilliant career opportunity and decided to be the James Dean of Movies whilst *continuing* to be the Elvis Presley of Rock 'n' Roll (way to go Elv'!).

Time to settle down with a bag of popcorn and check out some of the really great Presley pics you may have missed…

The Elivision multiplex

Now showing on SCREEN ONE:

Plot: It's the end of the American Civil War (1861–65). Elvis plays Clint Reno, whose eldest brother, Vance, has been killed in the scrapping. As Vance's beautiful girlfriend is looking a bit lonely and cheesed off, Elvis marries her. Then ... shucks, oh no! ... big bro' comes back! So he wasn't *completely* dead after all! Elvis feels *really* guilty about pinching his brother's girl ... *but*, despite this *and* all the kerfuffle that it causes, he still manages to sing some really nice songs ... including the title one, which was already top of the charts in real life. Vance finally gets killed whilst bravely defending his brother in a huge gunfight!

Behind the scenes: It was reported that Elvis was so excited about being in his first-ever movie that he not only memorized his own lines but took the trouble to learn everyone else's too! He also got acting and real life a bit confused. In one scene 'Clint' is getting all riled up and is determined to hang on to his gun, no matter what. He is so angry that he even ignores his mum when she tells him to drop it. However, when they got to this bit

99

in the rehearsals and Elvis's *film* mum said her line: 'Put that gun down, son!' Elvis immediately did as he was told. The director went bananas and asked Elvis what on earth he thought he was playing at. Elvis just looked a bit confused and replied that he'd dropped the gun because his 'mum' had told him to! Mmmph ... talk about a rebel without a clue!

The Tinseltown lowdown: There was a 50-foot-tall cardboard Elvis outside the New York cinema where the movie was first shown. (It didn't fool the fans though, they knew he was really 8 foot 10 inches.) When the movie opened at 8 o'clock in the morning on 15 November 1956, hundreds of Elvis-hungry teenagers were waiting to have their hero for breakfast. Even after the New York truant officers had pounced and dragged loads of them back to school, the queue was still 1,500 crazy Elvis fans long!

CALL OUT THE ARMY! THIS GIGANTIC ELVIS WILL DESTROY OUR CITY!

When the film went on general release Colonel Parker told all the cinema managers to check under the seats at the end of all performances to make sure no fans were hiding there. He was terrified they'd get to see the film a second time without paying!

Intermission: Old Super Ears

Learning his lines probably wasn't a problem for Elvis. He was said to have a brilliant memory and amazing powers of concentration. His pals called him 'Old Super Ears' because he could be talking to someone and listening to what other people were saying across the room at the same time. A friend said that he was once watching the 10 p.m. news with Elvis when he noticed he was 'echoing' what the newsman said, word for word. When he asked him how he could do this he said he'd seen the news at 6 p.m. and more or less remembered the whole lot. No wonder he amazed his mum and dad when he was little by remembering all the words of *all* the songs he ever heard on the radio!

Now showing on SCREEN TWO:

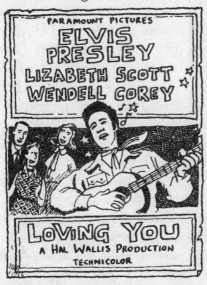

Plot: Country-boy truck-driver, Deke Rivers (played by Elvis, of course!) joins a hillbilly band, gets discovered by a pushy, ruthless agent and achieves rock 'n' roll fame. (Hmm ... *remind* you of anyone?) He fancies the agent *and* the singer in his band and gets in a tizzy over who to woo.

Behind the scenes: Gladys and Vernon went to see Elvis working on the film and were totally gobsmacked by glamorous Hollywood and the movie-world razzmatazz. Gladys later told her pals and rellies how 'her boy' had tons of people fussing round him, including someone to comb his hair, someone to help him get dressed ... *and* someone to ask if he was *'ready to work'*! Gladys was amazed that the directors just used about 20 extras to mill around for crowd scenes because she'd always thought that there really were at least 10 billion people in every one. (Oh! ... so *you* thought that too, did you?) In no time at all Glad and Vern each got themselves the mega-cool four-legged status symbol of the 1950s – a *poodle*!

Vernon called his Pierre and Gladys nick named hers 'Duke' after her fave actor, 'Duke' John Wayne, then made him wear a sissy little necklace collar with pretend diamonds in it. Vernon and Gladys actually appeared in *Loving You* as members of Deke's audience in the last bit of the film. After his mum died, Elvis couldn't bear to watch it because he found it too upsetting to see his number one fan gazing up at him with so much love in her eyes.

Intermission: 'Smellvis' Presley?

When Elvis went for his first screen test the Hollywood big shots said he had 'screen presence' and a real personal 'aura'. The receptionists at the film company are said to have noticed that he gave off another *sort* of aura, so powerful they had to press hankies to their noses. It was thought that

though Elvis always *looked* immaculate he didn't always *smell* immaculate and bathing wasn't his favourite pastime. Those receptionists weren't the only ones to notice El's smells. Someone who toured with him said that when he took off his socks the smell would fill the whole room and that he would just bung dirty undies and whatnot into his suitcase and then forget them ... or even just throw his dirty laundry away!

Now showing on SCREEN THREE:

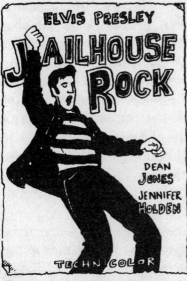

Plot: Vince Everett (Elvis) is bunged into jail for killing someone in a bar, so he passes his time by learning to sing and play the guitar. He comes out of jail and meets a beautiful music promoter who helps him become a top rock 'n' roll star (sounds sorta familiar, don't it?). After a bit (and quite uncharacteristically for a rock star) he gets all big-headed and unpleasant, has a punch up with Hunk, his old cell-mate, and ends up in hospital. This does him a world of good because when he gets better he turns into a real nice guy! Aah!

Interesting fact: On the wall of Elvis's 'jail cell' in the film there's a picture of Red Foley, the man who wrote 'Old Shep'. Well, I'll be doggone!

Behind the scenes: This film is really famous for its singing and dancing bits including the one in which the prisoners all escape but come straight back because the warden's giving a party that's just too much fun to miss. (American prisons are like that, people queue round the block just to get in them.)

Anyway, the high point of the scene is the 'Jailhouse Rock' number where the partying prisoners slide down a fireman's pole. During the rehearsals Elvis got really excited about this bit and just couldn't wait for his turn. However, when it came, he bunged himself down the pole so enthusiastically that he lost the artificial cap from one of his teeth.

He told the director that he could feel the cap rattling around inside his chest. Next minute, instead of being cool and creative movie-dudes like they were supposed to be, everyone was down on their hands and knees playing hunt the toothy-peg! They didn't find it but decided that Elvis had imagined the whole thing so they carried on rehearsing. But then Elvis told the director that one of his lungs had begun whistling! The noise he could hear turned out to be the tooth top which was trapped in his lung (he'd swallowed it and breathed in at the same time) and now it was sort of 'squeaking' every time Elvis breathed. He was immediately whipped off to hospital where a surgeon did a really tricky operation involving making a hole in Elvis's neck, parting his vocal cords (yes, *Elvis Presley's vocal cords!*) and fishing around in his lung for the tooth cap!

And, to cap it all, the film itself has a scene where Hunk punches Vince in the throat and he has to go hospital where everyone wonders if he'll ever sing again!

SNIFFLE!

GLAD IS SAD

What with all his mega-successful movies and records and whatnot, vast torrents of cash just kept pouring into Elvis's bulging bank accounts. So at last he was able to start buying his mum and dad the goodies he'd promised them, like a pair of matching pink Cadillacs, a new house, and some snazzy labour-saving gadgets...

One of the first things Elvis bought Gladys was a posh, newfangled automatic food-mixer. Not long afterwards he went and bought her *another* one! This puzzled the shop assistant no end so Elvis kindly explained to the dim bloke that Gladys had poorly legs and found walking to her new mixer really difficult so he thought he'd buy her *two* so that she could have one at each end of the worktop and not be forever hiking up and down the kitchen. Aaah ... what a thoughtful son!

Hanging out with the toffs

Unfortunately, having tons of money doesn't always bring happiness. It gets rid of old problems but occasionally brings new ones too. The people who lived near Glad and Vern's new house in Memphis weren't very happy about their famous neighbours. For a start they were dead sniffy about the fact that Gladys actually hung her washing outside on a washing line rather than drying it in a tumble drier. This quaint hillbilly custom might have been fine for the shanty towns of Tupelo but it certainly wasn't acceptable on a snobby new housing estate in Memphis.

But the thing that really annoyed them was the hordes of fans who hung around in the street all day and night hoping to catch a glimpse of 'The King' (as Elvis was now being called) on his visits home. When Gladys told Elvis that their snooty neighbours had actually got up a petition to get them to move out he was gobsmacked. Especially as the pesky Presley's were probably the only family in the whole street who actually *owned* their own house! So he had the great idea of buying all the *other* houses in the street and getting the *neighbours* to move out! Which they weren't too keen on. Anyway, the problem was solved by using lots more of Elvis's never-ending supply of dosh.

One day, while he was off being a megastar, Vern and Glad were cruising around Memphis in one of their pink Caddies when they spotted the most fantastic, beautiful, meganormous mansion for sale that had its own 18-acre grounds, *and* was also really handy for the shops! They fell in love with it, told Elvis about it, and soon afterwards he bought them this lil ol' shack known as…

Vern and Gladys were as pleased as punch with Graceland but with it being so big and posh and them being ex-hillbillies they decided that something which reminded them of their days back in Tupelo might make them feel more at home. So Vern got himself some hogs and Gladys decided to get a few chickens and whatnot. Elvis and his dad and one of the 'heavies' who were now

The Jungle Room

Pa's en suite hog pen

Mama's farm

minding 'the King' piled into his big yellow Cadillac then nipped off to a local farm where they bought a load of clucking, quacking, gobbling, honking creatures. But rather than doing the sensible thing and getting the farmer to deliver the birds, they loaded one turkey, two peacocks, eight ducks and twenty chickens into the back of the Cadillac, and set off for Graceland.

When they finally pulled into Graceland, Vernon and the minder were covered in bird poo and feathers, which tickled Gladys no end (the sight of the chaps that is, not the feathers).

In a similar poultry-gathering expedition Elvis went off and collected twenty geese in a Cadillac because he'd heard they loved to nibble grass and were really excellent for keeping your lawn trimmed.

Elvis is well wicked!

For every positive reaction there's a negative one. While millions of people were going crazy for Elvis, he drove others hopping mad! Grown-ups were really confused and worried by the way their teenage children reacted to him, especially when they screamed and rolled around on the floor at his concerts.

As a result, lots of people saw him as nothing but a big nuisance and ended up blaming many of society's problems on him … whether they were his fault or not.

Miami, USA, 1956 The Miami News accused Elvis of being the biggest freak in show business history. They said that he couldn't sing, couldn't play the guitar, couldn't dance and that each of his shows was attended by 2,000 idiots. (Apart from that they thought he was totally brilliant.)

Los Angeles, USA A posse of schoolgirls publicly burned a life-size picture of Elvis and said prayers in which they apologized to God for all the other *wicked* teenagers who worshipped him or tried to steal his shoelaces.

The Middle East In 1958 the Iranian government launched a 'Hate Elvis' campaign and banned his records from the radio. Rock 'n' roll was also banned in Egypt because doctors reported that too many teenagers were injuring their hips whilst dancing to it.

Southern states, USA The nasty racist organization known as the Klu Klux Klan visited cafés and bars in the southern states of America to check and see if there were any Elvis (or other rock 'n' roll records) on the jukeboxes. If there were, they told the owners to dump them.

Ottawa, Canada The headteacher of a convent school made an announcement over the loudspeaker system telling the apprentice nuns not to go to see the Elvis show that was coming to town in 1957. Every girl in the school had to write an oath on the blackboard promising to stay away from the concert. Eight naughty apprentice-nuns were caught and expelled after sneaking off to see the show.

Los Angeles, USA   A judge said that it was odd that every juvenile delinquent who came before him had an Elvis Presley haircut. He also said he wished Elvis had never been born.

All over the USA   When he first went on telly Elvis's wiggling pelvis and jiggling legs shocked loads of people. In 1957, not wishing to put people off their TV dinners, the telly bosses gave instructions that he was only to be filmed from the waist up.

Also in 1957, pop crooner and movie superstar Frank Sinatra said that rock 'n' roll was sung and played by 'cretinous goons'. At a press conference Elvis politely said that he admired Frank but that he shouldn't have said such things about rock 'n' roll.

Mexico The Mexican government were so scared that Elvis might cause riots that they banned him from entering their country.

Colorado, USA In 1959 the DJs at a radio station in Colorado decided to break all of their rock 'n' roll records (including lots by Elvis). They smashed one record every five minutes until their entire collection of 500 discs was destroyed.

Russia In 1958 Russia accused Elvis of being their Number One Public Enemy. They said that America was using him to wage 'psychological' warfare against them. In other words they were bothered that the Americans were planning to use Elvis to make young Russians discontented with their country and great way of life.

But more to the point, the Russians seemed to have overlooked one important fact!

GET LOST! HE CAN'T BE YOUR NUMBER ONE PUBLIC ENEMY! 'COS HE'S ALREADY OURS!

USA In October 1956 a church minister said that Elvis's body movements were vulgar and that he represented turmoil and confusion in American teenagers. Elvis had been brought up to be a 'good' boy and had regularly attended church throughout his childhood so when a reporter asked him how he felt after hearing that criticism from the church minister he replied...

That hurt me bitter. God gave me my voice. I never danced vulgar. I've just been jigglin'.

In the summer of 1956 Elvis was due to do another concert in Jacksonville, the place where he'd caused that huge stampede of fans the previous year when he'd invited them all to come backstage. The authorities were really worried that another riot would take place so the local judge told Elvis to cut down his body wiggling. Being a good boy, Elvis did exactly as he was told and stood fairly still for his performance. However, he did wiggle *his little finger* at the fans! His low-key pinky-jiggling drove the fans barmier than when he gave them the full works. Later on Elvis said that it made the girls scream the wildest he'd ever heard!

Positive-thinking Colonel Parker didn't let the 'Elvis bashers' faze him one bit. He just sold them all 'I Hate Elvis' badges then giggled all the way to the bank. However, one person who did get *really* upset by all the criticisms of Elvis was his mum, Gladys. She was a very religious woman and found the harsh comments from church leaders particularly upsetting. She would have loved to talk to Elvis about it all but nowadays he was always off touring or making films and records. As Elvis became more and more famous, poor Gladys sank deeper into the dumps.

A fan letter to Elvis – 1957

TO THE GREAT AND WONDERFUL 'ONE AND ONLY' ELVIS PRESLEY_ WHEREVER YOU ARE! x x x x

Dear Elvis,
I hope you don't mind me writin' to you like this but it seems like it is the only way I can get to speak to you proper, what with you whizzin' 'bout the country an' bein' surrounded by them pushy city folk all the time.
Elvis, I worship you. I am your number one fan. I think

you are the most wonderful human
being on God's earth. And I
__long__ to be close to you. I would
gladly give up my life for you.
You are breaking my heart (... but
I bet __all__ the girls say that to you).

I have followed your career right
from the start. The very start. And
I have seen your talent grow and
flower. Now you are tops... no
contest! And you know it? I
used to go to your concerts, but
not no more. That Colonel
Parker won't let me. So now I
only read about 'em in the papers.
Also in the papers I read the bad
stuff what people are sayin'.
That churns me up inside.
'Specially when it's church people
sayin' you're doin' the work of the
devil. 'Cos you were brought up
to be a __good__ boy. Both when
times was good... and when they
was bad! And believe me,
there was some __bad__ times.

Now I s'pose most folks would
say things are real good. For
you... __and__ for me. I got a big
ol' mansion. I got servants...

an' I got cotton-pickin' Mixmasters till they comin' out my ears!! But Elvis, I ain't happy. My life is empty. 'Cos I ain't got my itty-bitty boy no more!

Son (yes, it's me, your Mama, but I figure you may have guessed that!) I have lived my life just for _you._ But now you got the Colonel, an' the Guys, an' the girls. Boy... have you got <u>the girls</u>! Don't get me wrong, though son. I do like some of your girlfriends... 'specially that nice Dottie Harmony. But thing is, son, my life seems pointless now. All that work I did... was for you. Nothin' made me feel happier than to spend all mornin' baking your favourite coconut cake then see you sit at our big ol' kitchen table an' gobble the whole darn thing down in one go, or work my fingers to the bone in some ol' factory so I could buy you some candy or a toy. But now you don't need that. So I got nothin' to do. All I do is sit around this mansion worrying you'll be in a wreck or them fans will tear you to pieces.

Elvis... sometimes I wish ~~that~~... <u>we was poor again</u>! In a shack next to our good ol' neighbours. An' best of all... back to bein' a loving little family of three! What I would really like is for you to give up your rock 'n' roll and open a nice little furniture store here in Memphis. And then get married. But that would be for me. And it is <u>your</u> life, son. And I only want what is best for <u>you</u>. And what makes <u>you</u> happy.

♡ Hugs and kisses

x Your ever lovin' Mama xxx

PS 'Scuse the tear stains.

PPS I have got you some of them special pork chops what you love so much. I thought I'd cook 'em up for you with a mess of greens outa my little garden. But I don't know when you're comin' home next.

HIS LATEST FLAME: DOTTIE HARMONY

Elvis first spotted Dottie at a nightclub where she was a dancer. He sent his buddies to chat her up for him but she told them to get lost so he kneeled at her feet and told her she was the most beautiful woman in the world! That did the trick and she went out with him. He told her to stop smoking and she said she would ... if Elvis would stop biting his nails! When she flew to Memphis to spend Christmas with Elvis and his parents, there were girls at the airport screaming and waving 'GO HOME DOTTIE HARMONY!' banners. While she was there, Elvis read the Bible to her every night and they rode around Memphis in matching motorcycle outfits. A real cool couple! They went shopping and Elvis bought a little monkey which sat on Dottie's knee on the way home and did some monkey business on her white dress. They stopped at a petrol station so she could clean up but the monkey got free in the washroom and caused chaos! Never a dull moment with EP.

Glad gets even sadder

On nearly all of the photographs taken of her between 1956 and 1958 Gladys looks really unhappy. You'd think she'd be delighted, wouldn't you? She'd gone from being incredibly poor to living in a huge mansion in its own grounds. And she'd seen her only son become the richest and most famous entertainer in the world. Most people would say that she ought to have been the proudest and happiest mum in the world! But she wasn't. And just when it seemed like she couldn't get any more fed up something happened to make her think she might lose Elvis for ever. He was called up into the American army!

G.I. BLUES

When everyone discovered that Elvis had got to join the army, the whole world was gobsmacked. The only people who didn't seem put out were cool and calculating Colonel Tom, the Elvis copy-cat pop stars, who suddenly realized they had a chance to fill the chart gaps he was going to be leaving empty, and lots of boyfriends who hoped their Elvis-crazy girlfriends would start paying them some attention again.

Elvis himself wasn't too happy about swapping his perfect pop paradise for parade-ground purgatory but he decided to put a brave face on it because he had no choice (and the Colonel had told him to anyway!).

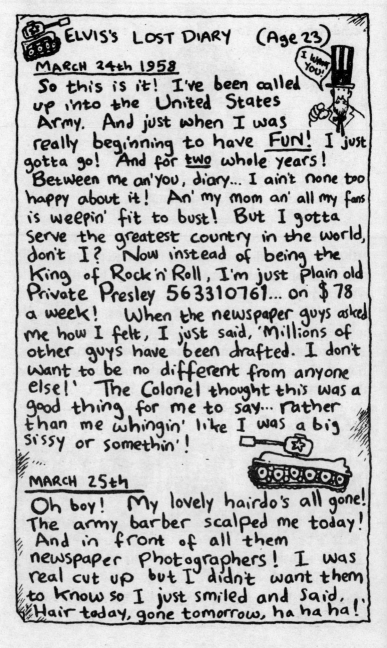

ELVIS'S LOST DIARY (Age 23)

MARCH 24th 1958

So this is it! I've been called up into the United States Army. And just when I was really beginning to have **FUN!** I just gotta go! And for **two** whole years! Between me an' you, diary... I ain't none too happy about it! An' my mom an' all my fans is weepin' fit to bust! But I gotta serve the greatest country in the world, don't I? Now instead of being the King of Rock 'n' Roll, I'm just plain old Private Presley 563310761... on $78 a week! When the newspaper guys asked me how I felt, I just said, 'Millions of other guys have been drafted. I don't want to be no different from anyone else!' The Colonel thought this was a good thing for me to say... rather than me whingin' like I was a big sissy or somethin'!

MARCH 25th

Oh boy! My lovely hairdo's all gone! The army barber scalped me today! And in front of all them newspaper photographers! I was real cut up but I didn't want them to know so I just smiled and said, 'Hair today, gone tomorrow, ha ha ha!'

122

and they all laughed too. Cool under pressure... that's me!

Before → 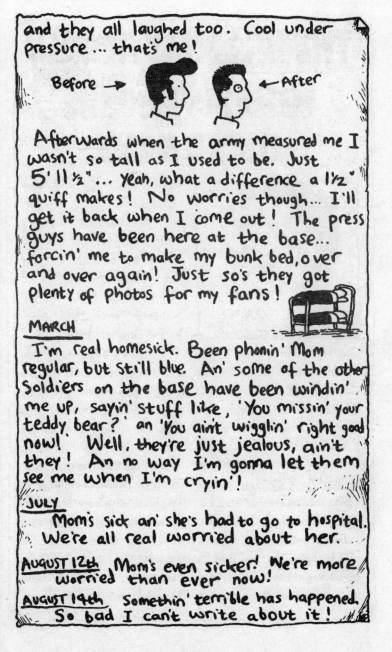 ← After

Afterwards when the army measured me I wasn't so tall as I used to be. Just 5'11½"... yeah, what a difference a 1½" quiff makes! No worries though... I'll get it back when I come out! The press guys have been here at the base... forcin' me to make my bunk bed, over and over again! Just so's they got plenty of photos for my fans!

MARCH

I'm real homesick. Been phonin' Mom regular, but still blue. An' some of the other soldiers on the base have been windin' me up, sayin' stuff like, 'You missin' your teddy bear?' an 'You aint wigglin' right good now!' Well, they're just jealous, ain't they! An no way I'm gonna let them see me when I'm cryin'!

JULY

Mom's sick an' she's had to go to hospital. We're all real worried about her.

AUGUST 12th
Mom's even sicker! We're more worried than ever now!

AUGUST 14th
Somethin' terrible has happened. So bad I can't write about it!

THE HILLBILLY HERALD

August 15th 1958

MEMPHIS MOURNS ELVIS'S MAMA

Gladys Love Presley (46), mother of Elvis Aaron Presley (23), is dead. Gladys took ill t'other week and was rushed to Memphis hospital where she passed away with husband Vernon at her bedside an' her beloved pink Cadillac parked where she could see it from her bed. Some say it was drink killed her and some say it was a broken heart but the doctors say it was really her liver that was broke. (An' them hot-shot medics sure know what they talkin' 'bout!) Elvis, her only son, has definitely got a broken heart. Him and his poor ol' daddy have been sittin' on the steps of Graceland sobbin' their cotton pickin' socks off an' wanderin' around the place lookin' completely lost.

As Gladys's body lay at rest in Graceland 3,000 people walked past it and paid their respects. It's reported that Elvis looked down at his mama and sobbed, 'Mama I'd give up every dime I own and go back to diggin' ditches just to have you back.' Gladys was a good, decent and kind woman who never had a bad word for anyone. She always did her best for her son and husband. May she rest in peace.

🐁 ELVIS'S LOST DIARY (Age 23-24)

AUGUST 25th 1958

Everyone's been trying to cheer me up after what happened to Mama. The Tennessee Highway Patrol even took me for a ride in one of their helicopters. And let me drive it for a bit. Now that was fun. And I've had more than 100,000 cards and letters from my fans saying they're sorry 'bout what happened! I reckon they must really love me! Wherever would I be without 'em!?

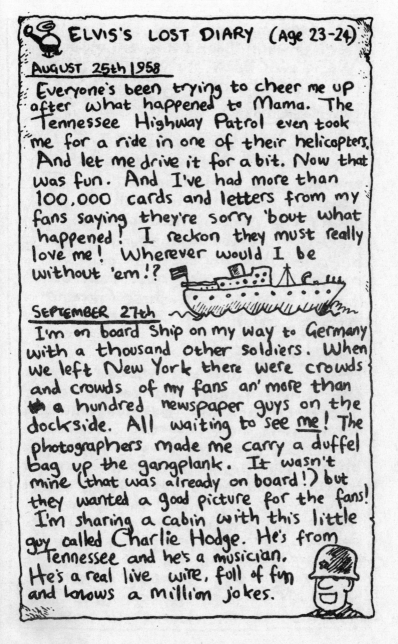

SEPTEMBER 27th

I'm on board Ship on my way to Germany with a thousand other soldiers. When we left New York there were crowds and crowds of my fans an' more than a hundred newspaper guys on the dockside. All waiting to see <u>me</u>! The photographers made me carry a duffel bag up the gangplank. It wasn't mine (that was already on board!) but they wanted a good picture for the fans! I'm sharing a cabin with this little guy called Charlie Hodge. He's from Tennessee and he's a musician. He's a real live wire, full of fun and knows a million jokes.

He's keepin' me entertained and stoppin' me from thinkin' 'bout Mama too much! We've even been playing some country music for the other guys on board.

NOVEMBER 1958

My officers say I'm a real good trooper! And hey! I keep winning 'Best Dressed Soldier' award... every month! Well what's the point of having millions of dollars if you don't spend 'em! Spit polishin' my boots an' pressin' my pants keeps the guys real busy too! What's more these German gals sure go for my cool threads!

JANUARY 1959

Oops! Me an' the guys sorta got the whole family thrown out of the Hotel Grunewald. But we only been havin' fun: havin' water pistol fights an' wrestling in the hallways, playin' the piano an' singin all night long... S'nothin' to get miffed about! Anyway we was havin' this shavin' cream fight an' Red was chasin' me so I locked myself in my room an' Red set fire to some paper an' shoved it under my door tryin' to smoke

126

me out. Well, the hotel boss didn't take kindly to this and that's why we're all movin' out to a little house what we're gonna rent.

FEBRUARY 1960

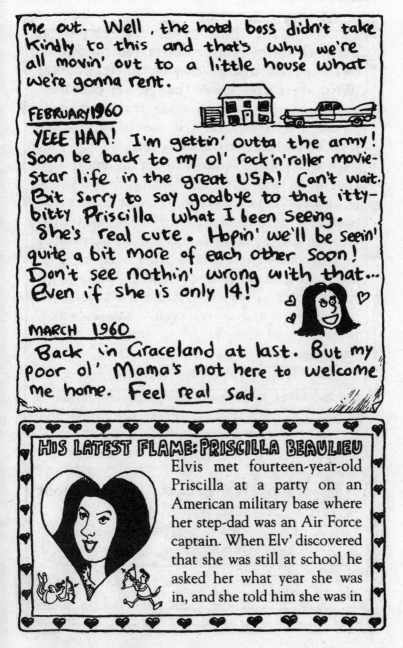

YEEE HAA! I'm gettin' outta the army! Soon be back to my ol' rock'n'roller movie-star life in the great USA! Can't wait. Bit sorry to say goodbye to that itty-bitty Priscilla what I been seeing.

She's real cute. Hopin' we'll be seein' quite a bit more of each other soon! Don't see nothin' wrong with that... Even if she is only 14!

MARCH 1960

Back in Graceland at last. But my poor ol' Mama's not here to welcome me home. Feel <u>real</u> sad.

HIS LATEST FLAME: PRISCILLA BEAULIEU

Elvis met fourteen-year-old Priscilla at a party on an American military base where her step-dad was an Air Force captain. When Elv' discovered that she was still at school he asked her what year she was in, and she told him she was in

127

the ninth grade (year nine). He was so amazed that he started laughing, and cheesed her off by saying, 'Why, you're just a baby'. Then he introduced her to his gran while he ate five huge bacon sarnies all slathered with mustard. (He was famous for his sophisticated chat up techniques.)

After Elvis left Germany he kept in touch with Priscilla and a bit later on she went to live with him at Graceland but they didn't actually get married until 1967. The wedding caused loads of bad feeling amongst Elvis's old mates and bodyguards because most of them weren't invited to the ceremony. One of them was so miffed that he said he'd never work for Elvis again then sulked in his hotel room and missed the fabulous reception nosh-up which included a suckling pig, fried chickens, oysters, champagne and a six-tier wedding cake studded with tiny pearls and pink hearts.

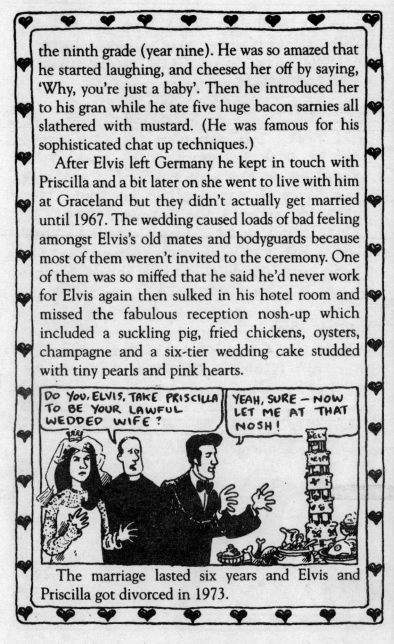

The marriage lasted six years and Elvis and Priscilla got divorced in 1973.

128

EL'S ANGELS

While Elvis was in the army he had a few buddies with him who kept him company and did odd jobs for him. They weren't soldiers, they were members of his personal 'boys' gang' who were known as the 'Guys', or 'The Memphis Mafia', because quite a few were rellies or old buddies from Memphis. Between the time he got out of the army in 1960 and his death in 1977 he more or less kept his 'Mafia' around him all the time. They did everything for him, including giving round-the-clock protection, keeping him cheerful *and* 'taking care of business' in general.

1 To die for the King

As soon as Elvis began to get famous everyone worried that someone would try to harm him in some way. Maybe a boyfriend, driven mad with jealousy by his sweetheart constantly going on about how she loved Elvis, would try to shoot him! Or perhaps a girl who was completely gone on Elvis would be so envious of his *real* girlfriends that she would attempt to ruin his good looks by giving him an enormous false nose transplant while he was fast asleep.

To guard against this sort of possibility the 'Guys' stayed really close to Elvis and always carried guns so they could blast a would-be assassin to bits. It more or less went without saying that if someone did try to do something terrible to the King it was the Guys' job to hurl themselves instantly between him and the danger, no matter what it was: fists, bullets, knives ... they had to take it all on the chin!

2 To diet for the King

Elvis found it difficult to to keep his figure trim so he often went on diets to fight the flab. Sometimes he would just eat one particular sort of food such as yoghurt or alfalfa (healthy veggie stuff) for weeks on end in the hope that he'd become slim as one of his blue suede shoelaces again. Dieting isn't easy – especially if everyone around you is noshing fit to bust! So when Elvis slimmed, *everyone* slimmed! If the King ate yoghurt until it came out of his ears all the Guys had to eat yoghurt until it came out of *their* ears! It was also the job of the guys to hide food from Elvis when he was on a diet ... and to get shouted at when he couldn't find it!

3 To look after the King's pickles
In 1970 a drummer called Jerry Carrigan went to beat his bongoes at one of Elvis's studio recording-sessions. Just as Jerry was feeling a bit peckish he noticed one of the minders bring an enormous container of pickled cucumbers into the studio. He saw one or two of the 'Guys' help themselves to the pickles and thought something like, 'Hmm scrumptious, I'm ready for a snack!' and went over to get a couple of gherkins for himself. As

he reached into the container one of Elvis's bodyguards gave Jerry a really threatening look then growled...

4 To keep the King *out* of pickles
The more famous Elvis became, the more likely he was to be mobbed (and possibly torn to pieces!) by his crazed fans. They didn't hate him, they just wanted a bit of him for themselves. So the Guys had to think up more and more elaborate ways of protecting him. When he was working on one particular film in New Orleans and wanted to return to his hotel he was driven through the city lying on the floor of a battered old car in the hope that no one would realize he was in it. He couldn't actually go directly to the hotel because it was besieged by fans so the Guys strung a series of rope-ladders from rooftop to rooftop so he could get to it from a nearby building then shimmy down the fire escape and into his bedroom window without being spotted!

5 To *look* the business
When Elvis first went to Hollywood he took the Guys with him. Apart from looking cool and guarding Elvis there wasn't much for them to do. In order to give everyone the impression that they were busy and important people with a real purpose in life – rather than

(as some people thought) layabouts sponging off their old mate who just happened to have become an international mega-star (perish the thought!) – they all got dark glasses, dressed in dark suits and carried briefcases. (You can't beat a briefcase for making a 'nobody' look like a 'somebody'.) They didn't actually carry much in the cases. It was reported that Elvis's cousin, Gene Smith, only carried a hairbrush and a doorknob in his.

6 To '*take care of business*' (and wear '*the badge*'!)
Elvis gave each of the Mafia a 14-carat gold necklace from which dangled a really tasteful and restrained 'medallion'. The medallion was engraved with a Captain-Marvel-style lightning bolt and the initials TCB which stood for Taking Care of Business (...and not Totally Cruddy Badge).

7 To take care of the King while he *does* his business!
Whenever Elvis visited the 'comfort station' to have a tiddle or whatever (yes, mega-stars do do that sort of thing!) he was accompanied by his minders. They didn't actually go into the cubicle with him but they did bar anyone else from entering the Gents while the King was doing his stuff.

Rude bit (only to be read by over-12s): The Mafia had a naughty nickname that actually referred to the fact that they more or less did 'everything' for Elvis. It was 'the fart catchers' – so maybe *that's* what they were doing when they accompanied him to the loo!?

8 To be fun to be with ... but not *too* brainy!
During the early 1960s a reporter once 'suggested' to Elvis that his minders weren't what you'd call 'intellectuals' (brainy bods) and wondered if he might occasionally wish for the sort of mates he could have some stimulating conversation with ... or even *learn* something from! Elvis didn't take kindly to this and replied that he didn't want a group of 'intellectuals' around him. He said that as you only had one life it was important to surround yourself with people you could have some fun with. (Then he tweaked the reporter's nose and asked him if he fancied a game of tag.)

9 To stay awake all night long!
Elvis loved movies, but didn't start watching them before midnight! He hired the local cinema to watch the films and would make everyone keep him company as he enjoyed the flicks until the early hours of the morning. If the film got boring he made the projectionist 'fast

forward' but when it got to a part that he *really* liked he made them rewind so he could watch the same scene over and over again, maybe as many as six times in a row! Sometimes the Guys became bored stiff by this and fell asleep. If Elvis heard anyone snoring he'd tell one of the *other* Guys to find out who it was and wake them up!

10 To always be '*cool*'!

The one thing that Elvis demanded from his Guys was *complete* loyalty. He was an international mega-star and the world's journalists were desperate to find out about every tiny single detail of his life so they could spill the beans to the millions of people who wanted to read about him. Elvis once told one of his minders that they would be friends for a '*long time*' as long as he was '*cool*'. This meant that Elvis didn't ever want him tittle-tattling or passing on juicy gossip about Elvis's intimate personal life to the newspapers ... like whether he cleaned his teeth before or *after* he washed his face, or if he put on his right sock first or his left one ... that sort of thing! Unfortunately, during the 1970s, two of Elvis's longest-serving bodyguards betrayed him by going off and co-writing a book about some of his less attractive habits. This may have had something to do with the fact that Elvis's dad had just sacked them!

Meet some of the Guys

1 Lamar Fike – a.k.a. 'Bull' Fike, Buddha, or the Great Speckled Bird
Elvis took a liking to Lamar because he made him laugh. He was also rather plump (he weighed 350 lbs) and no doubt standing next to him made Elvis feel better about his own weight problems. When Elvis was bunged in the army Lamar tried to join up with him but the army decided there was too much of him. It's said that Lamar once fell off the toilet at Graceland and became wedged between the seat and the wall so the fire brigade had to be called to rescue him. As well as being chum, class clown, court jester and minder it was Lamar's job to sort out the lighting for Elvis's stage shows.

2 Robert West a.k.a. 'Red' West

Red West was a big, tough football player who was called Red because he had red hair (rather than 'ginger bonce' … which could have got you a thrashing). Red first met Elvis when they were at school together. Elvis was in the boys' loo being bullied by some yobbo classmates who didn't appreciate the fashion statements he was making. Just as the thugs were about to give Elvis the short-back-and-sides he didn't want Red walked in and saved the day.

After this, Red became Elvis's friend. Red didn't know it at the time but one day protecting Elvis from possible attacks by thugs and maniacs every time he visited the loo would become part of his full-time career. He actually said he thought that Elvis was a 'nobody' when they were at school and that he felt really sorry for him because he seemed really lonely and had no friends. When he first heard him singing on the radio he was completely gobsmacked and said, 'It was bigger than life!' Red was always ready for action and acted as a stuntman in stacks of Elvis's films.

3 Gene Smith

Gene was Elvis's cousin and before Elvis hit the big-time he'd also been his factory workmate in Memphis. When Elvis found fame and fortune he made Gene his chauffeur and when he was in Hollywood working on his movies Gene had the job of looking after the King's clothes – making sure his shoes were shined, shirts pressed, socks fed, trousers taken for walks ... that sort of thing. Not a particularly exhausting sort of job you might say. Well, when someone asked Gene what he actually did for a living he replied...

> *I don't do anythin' ... I'm Elvis's cousin!*

4 Charlie Hodge

Elvis made friends with Charlie when they were both in the army. Charlie was also from Tennessee and was a gospel singer, country musician and great joke-teller. As you know, him and Elvis shared a ship's cabin just after Elvis's mum had died and Charlie kept him cheerful. Not long after they'd come out of the army Charlie visited Elvis at Graceland. After the visit Elvis and the Guys were just about to make a train trip to Hollywood when Elvis asked Charlie if he fancied going and Charlie said: 'Why not', and that was that. He remained a Memphis Mafian until Elvis died. Sometimes Charlie played guitar on stage with Elvis and also handed him his scarves (which Elv' bunged to ecstatic fans) and his Gatorade (Elv's fizzy drink, not medication for sick reptiles) while he was performing.

The Guys in action – well, sort of...

During the late 1960s Elvis and a whole bunch of top celebs began to get *really* worried about their personal safety after a film star, Sharon Tate, and some of her pals got murdered by evil maniac, Charles Manson, and some of *his* pals. Elvis began wearing a bullet-proof vest every time he went on stage!

Then, in August 1970, an anonymous caller said Elvis would be murdered while he was performing. Ooer! Elvis immediately surrounded himself with wall to wall Guys. And just to make *completely* sure he wasn't wasted mid-wiggle, the police and the FBI were brought in too. On the day of the show there were plain-clothes cops in the audience, a doctor was waiting backstage with emergency supplies of oxygen and blood and an ambulance was parked outside!

A few moments before he was due to go out on stage (for the last time ever?) Elvis sat in his dressing-room sobbing his sequins off and saying final goodbyes to his dad and the Mafia. In between sobs he managed to tell the Guys that if some big 'nuisance' (actually, that wasn't *quite* the word he used) tried to kill him he wanted them to 'rip his eyes out'. Cripes!

With the Guys crouched behind loudspeakers and guns stuck inside his boots and down the top of his trousers, Elvis finally went on stage. The tension was tremendous! Things went fine until, in the middle of the show, a man on the balcony stood up and yelled 'ELVIS!' Oh no! Elvis immediately dropped to one knee like they do in the cop movies and said 'Yeah?' and the man said 'Can you sing, "Don't Be Cruel"?' So Elvis did, and everyone went ... 'PHEW!' And that was that! The King lived to wiggle another day! Someone who'd been there that night said that Elvis actually seemed a bit *disappointed* that he'd finished the show without even one single bullet-hole in him!

ELVIS'S LOST DIARY (Age 25)

MARCH 26th 1960

Hardly been back five seconds an' it's all Elvis-a-go-go! Just been the special guest of honour on lil ol' Frank Sinatra's 'Welcome Home Elvis' TV show. Yeah him!... Frank Sinatra! The same guy who badmouthed me just a couple of years ago! Well, seems like you gotta have at least fourteen faces if you wanna get on in showbiz! I'll go with that! 'Specially as they're payin' me $125,000 for a six minute TV appearance!

WELCOME BACK ELVIS... WE LOVE YOU!

FRANK

JUMPED UP ROCK 'N' ROLL GOON!

WHY THANKS OL' BUDDY

WRINKLY OLD CROONER

ME

APABIL 18th

I'm back in the army! 'Cos I'm on my way to California to shoot GI Blues, my new movie. Certainly had plenty of rehearsals for it these past two years... ha ha! Me an' the Guys got us two private luxury coaches on the train. Huge crowds at all the stations all the way. To see me! Feel like royalty... me, King Elvis!

APRIL 21ST

We're here. When we got to LA the train had to pull into a siding so's me an the Guys could sneak off. Otherwise there'd've been another riot!

APRIL 27th

Got me another number one in the charts. 'Stuck on you': another million seller. Shoot! S'all just like before I went in the army. Everythin' hot 'n' happenin' for E.P!

MAY 1960

Holy mackerel! Had me some visitors today. I get 'em on the movie set most every day, but this was somethin' else! There was the King and Queen of Thailand, the

PTO→

141

President of Brazil's wife and her daughter, plus a load of showbiz stars too. And oh yeah, how could I forget them three princesses from Scandinavia. I went down on my knees and sung them lovely ladies a song. Well, they may be royalty, but underneath they're just cute chicks, ain't they? Shoot! All them top folk in one day! An' me just a lil ol' hillbilly truck driver from Tennessee. Somehow I sorta think I'm gettin' even more famous than ever!

June 1960

Between my filmin' sessions me an' the Guys have been havin' us a ball! Last night we chased around and around the hotel corridors squirtin' each

Other with water pistols. And after that we had us a real goofy game of hide an' seek! My Memphis buddies are just so much <u>fun</u>!

Fun fun fun!
Elvis really did find time to goof around between making all those films and records. And of course, the rough, tough Guys were the perfect companions for...

1 Knock 'n' roller skating
When he was a kid Elvis could hardly afford to go to the roller-skating rink known as the Rainbow Rollerdrome but when he got famous he just rented out the whole place so him and his pals could have wild skating parties with free ice-cream, free drinks and free skating gear for all (except Elvis, of course). They'd all turn up at midnight, tog themselves up in padded clothing then split into two teams and play the gentle and thoughtful game that Elvis was said to have invented. When his wacky cousin, Junior Smith, blew his ref's whistle, everyone went bananas. They didn't need a ball or goals, because the game was ... *war!* As the Rollerdrome organ

belted out Elvis's favourite music, everyone belted everyone else! So it was a good thing there was a first-aid team on hand, wasn't it? The other game they played was the Whip. A chain of thirty skaters would whizz around the rink with the one in the centre going the slowest and the one on the end going at 30 mph. And of course, it was the one on the end who occasionally flew off the handle!

2 Fairy-tale fairgrounds

Elvis loved fairgrounds, especially as he'd scored his first singing success at the Tupelo one by winning $5 for his famous dead-dog song. Now that he had slightly *more* than $5 in his piggy bank he hired the Memphis Fairgrounds for fun whenever he felt like it. His favourite ride was the roller-coaster which he always rode standing in the front car.

3 Football

Elvis was crazy about American football and had his own mates 'n' minders team who played matches against other 'celebs'. When Elvis was older and out of condition he found footy a bit of a pain. It was reported that he would sometimes get the ball and begin running with it, then wouldn't be able to stop and would go charging on like a steam-engine until he crashed into a wall.

4 Firework battles

Sometimes Elvis's idea of a cracking good time was irresponsible to say the least, especially the firework-throwing 'battles' he had with the Guys. One of these took place on New Year's Eve 1972. Thirty-seven-year-old Elvis and his eleven *grown-up* pals put on heavily padded clothing, goggles, thick gloves and American football helmets, then went into his huge garden where he divided them into two teams and handed out more than a thousand dollars'-worth of fireworks. The two 'armies' got themselves tooled up with Roman candles, bangers, 'bombs', skyrockets, jumping jacks ... the lot! They then went to war, racing around and throwing

fireworks at each other for as long as two or three hours! Thankfully, because they were wearing protective clothing, no one ever got seriously hurt or killed but at the end of the battle the air was full of smoke and their clothing (and occasionally their skin) was scorched and full of holes.

Really really important words of warning!! NEVER attempt to copy this stupid idea. At times Elvis and the Guys were more childish than children. He really was a mass of contrasts – on the one hand he'd be polite, well-behaved and get everyone's admiration and respect ... and on the other he'd act like a big twit!

5 Racing anything he could could get his hands on
Elvis liked to charge around on enormous motorbikes
with the Guys. It's reported that the local Memphis
police sometimes closed the highway in the middle of
the night so that they could race their bikes. When they
weren't racing they went
cruising around Memphis.
Elvis always had to be at
the front of the pack. If
one of the Guys wanted to
talk to him they were
allowed to come alongside
and have a couple of
quick words but then they
had to drop back again.

As well as the motorbikes Elvis raced anything else
that had wheels, including dune buggies (in California),
slot cars (he had a giant raceway at Graceland), golf-
carts and go-karts. Once, just for a laugh, and to give the
crowds of gawping fans a scare, he raced his go-kart at
the gates of Graceland but didn't manage to brake in
time. Fortunately the only thing hurt was the gates!
Perhaps he should have renamed Graceland ... Raceland!

6 Monkeying around
Elvis had a brilliant sense of humour. His fave TV show
was *Monty Python* and he could reel off whole sketches
by heart. He also played *hundreds* of practical jokes on
people. Here's a selection of the most chucklesome:
• A band leader called Joe Guercio was providing the
  backing music for Elvis at a nightclub. One of Elvis's
  minders asked him what it was like working with Elvis

and Joe replied, 'It's like following a marble falling down concrete steps!' In other words, musically speaking, he was hard to keep up with. The minder told Elvis what Joe had said. The next day when Joe went to his dressing-room he couldn't get the door open. After lots of pushing and shoving he did get it open a smidge and discovered about 3,000 marbles on the floor with a note stuck on his mirror saying:

- There was always a crowd of fans hanging around the big electric gates of Graceland in the hope that they'd catch a glimpse of their hero. Elvis once told his cousin Harold to open the gates so they could all come in and see him. Harold did as he was asked and the fans began to wander up the drive expecting to meet Elvis. In the meantime Elvis nipped out of the back gates and then Harold closed the front gates behind the fans so that they were all locked in. A few moments later Elvis appeared outside the front gates in his car, gave his astonished admirers a friendly wave and drove off up the road. Unlike modern mega-stars who would have probably just boiled the captive fans in oil then fed them to their pet crocodiles, Elvis came back and had a chat to them. Because the last thing he wanted to do was upset his fans. Aaah! What a *nice* mega-star!

- The moment they arrived at a hotel, Elvis and the Guys moved all the furniture out of his room and hid it in a corridor, then called the room-service waiter and complained that they'd arrived to find an empty room. While the waiter was fetching the manager they put the furniture back in the room as quickly as they could. When the poor bloke returned with the manager he looked a right Charlie!

- Just before they were due to arrive at a posh party, handsome Elvis and his glamorous girlfriend blacked out their front teeth. After making their grand entrance with their mouths closed tight they began grinning at all the guests, who of course were totally 'gobsmacked'!

7 More monkeying around (...with a monkey!)
After sharing a TV show with some performing apes, Elvis bought himself a little chimpanzee called Scatter. Scatter was an extremely cheeky chimp who got up to all sorts of monkey-business including:

- Getting drunk and ripping out all the phonelines in a house that Elvis was renting.

- Waggling his naughty bits at complete strangers. Wonder who he learnt *that* from!

- Driving Elvis's Rolls Royce. One of the minders got Scatter a peaked chauffeur's cap and sat him on his knee as he drove the car around Memphis. Whenever he saw anyone who looked like they were in need of a heart attack he ducked down and left Scatter holding the wheel.

• Biting people. He bit Elvis's step-mother and some years later he bit one of his maids. Not long after this he was found dead in his cage (and at supper that evening the cheeseburgers tasted sort of ... *different*). Some years after Scatter died Elvis was reported to have said, 'Scatter was one of the best buddies I ever had!'

THE COMEBACK KID

After he'd come out of the army Elvis's life settled into a pattern of having fun with his buddies, making movies, getting lots of money for doing it, then having lots *more* fun with the Guys (not to mention quite a few Girls!). This went on for almost all of the 1960s but as the decade decayed, so did Elvis's happiness. He was sick of churning out films where he sang to dogs, or girls, or horses or guys he was beating up! He knew they weren't very creative or original and weren't even a laugh to do any more. He hadn't done a live concert for ages and there were tons of great new acts around like the Rolling Stones and the Beatles who were making him look like a real past-his-wiggle-by-date pop dinosaur.

150

Then Colonel Tom had an idea…

ELVIS's LOST DIARY (Age 33 - 34)

8th JANUARY 1968

I'm 33 today! I got 33 gold discs to my name. My movies've made more than $135 million. I got more money than ever… it just keeps pouring in. But I'm completely fed up! My films are boring! I ain't had a top ten hit since '65. I aint done a live show since I was 26! An the newspapers are calling me an ol' has-been. So the Colonel and some TV guys are gonna try and kick start my music career with a TV Comeback Special. They're gonna pay me a quarter of a million dollars for it. Well, diary, between you, me an' this pen, I'm <u>scared</u>! Maybe my fans won't love me no more! An' if they don't… I reckon that'll really be the <u>end</u> of me!

1ST FEBRUARY

YIPPEEE! I'm happy today! Why? Because I'm a <u>daddy</u>! This afternoon, at one minute past five, me and Priscilla had a little girl. We're gonna call her Lisa Marie. The

Marie's after Colonel Parker's wife. Wonder what the future holds for my little girl?

10TH MARCH

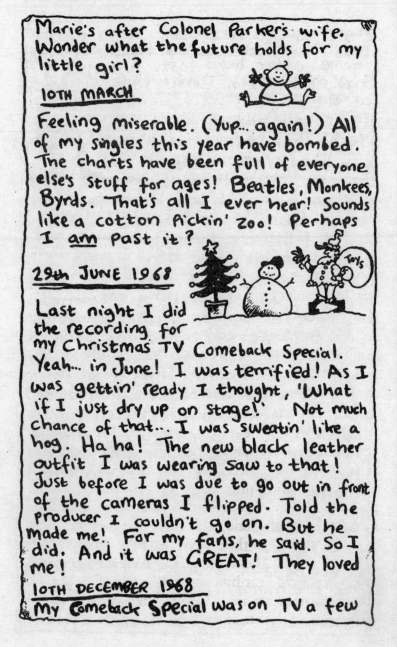

Feeling miserable. (Yup... again!) All of my singles this year have bombed. The charts have been full of everyone else's stuff for ages! Beatles, Monkees, Byrds. That's all I ever hear! Sounds like a cotton pickin' zoo! Perhaps I __am__ past it?

29th JUNE 1968

Last night I did the recording for my Christmas TV Comeback Special. Yeah... in June! I was terrified! As I was gettin' ready I thought, 'What if I just dry up on stage!' Not much chance of that... I was sweatin' like a hog. Ha ha! The new black leather outfit I was wearing saw to that! Just before I was due to go out in front of the cameras I flipped. Told the producer I couldn't go on. But he made me! For my fans, he said. So I did. And it was GREAT! They loved me!

10TH DECEMBER 1968

My Comeback Special was on TV a few

nights ago. It was a hit! A guy in the papers said that I had 'found my way home' after being lost. And that I had made my old songs sound as fresh as though they were written yesterday! My records have started sellin' again! Yeah! Way to go! Feelin' good! Happy new year!

Welcome to my wardrobe(s)

Elvis was really fussy about his appearance and as a teenager he would spend ages with his nose pressed against the window of Lansky's, the coolest clothes shop in Memphis, wishing he could own some of the snazzy threads on display. But unfortunately, as he had even *less* dosh than an unemployed money-spider, Elvis would just go away with nothing but a head full of fashion dreams (and a flat nose). Years later, the Lansky brothers recalled that even though young Elvis wore shabby clothes he always had real great hair and nice manners! Which both came a whole lot cheaper than the clothes in Lansky's. When he started his first job Elvis was really chuffed because the Lanskys told him that he could have some clothes from them, then give them just one dollar a week until the things were paid for. Their kindness paid off, though, because years later Elvis ended up spending so much money with them that they were able to double the size of their shop.

The way Elvis dressed was part of creating the cool image that would get him noticed, so as well as lugging musical instruments around to his various gigs he had to cart masses of clothes around too. He was once so upset after accidentally leaving a whole suitcase full of clothes at a petrol station that he cried all the way home.

When he became a millionaire Elvis kept wardrobes full of identical clothes in three different homes in three different cities. So if he happened to fly from Memphis to Los Angeles absentmindedly wearing just *one* of his favourite pink socks, it wouldn't be a problem because its identical-twin cousins would be there waiting for him!

Dress your own Elvis

Note – For the sake of decency, the illustrator has quite rightly and properly dressed the Elvii (plural of Elvis) in rather fetching boxer shorts. However, according to one clothes designer, he never ever wore underpants!

154

EARLY 50s ELVIS

BAGGY PINK JACKET WITH SEQUINS AND BLACK 'TEAR-DROPS' SEWN INTO IT (PROBABLY BY GLADYS)

BLACK SHIRT AND WHITE TIE

BLACK 'PEG-TOP' TROUSERS WITH PINK SEAM DOWN LEG

This outfit is the sort of stuff Elvis wore when he was a young style-warrior and rock 'n' roller in fifties Memphis. He'd buy most of this gear from Lansky's, although his mum did knock him up the occasional snazzy shirt. At this time in America these sorts of clothes were generally worn by black men. Snooty white teenagers and fuddy-duddy grown-ups looked down on Elvis for copying the styles of people whom they considered to be their inferiors. However, Elvis had the last laugh because the moment he achieved nationwide fame, thousands of teenagers of all skin shades were desperately trying to copy the 'new' Elvis Presley look.

GOLD LAMÉ ELVIS

GOLD LAMÉ SUIT

Colonel Parker and Elvis's record company gave him this bobby dazzler in 1957 as a way of saying 'Thank you, slurp, fondle, cringe, cringe' for the Amazon of dosh that was roaring and tumbling into their bank accounts all because of him. Lamé is material like cotton or wool with threads of metal woven through it. So guess what metal was woven through this suit! (Brainy readers only to attempt this question.) The suit, which cost

GOLD STRING TIE

GOLDEN SHOES

GOLD LACES WITH RHINESTONES (HILLBILLY DIAMONDS)

$10,000, matched Elvis's gold Cadillac and was designed by Nudie Cohen of Nudie's Rodeo Tailors, Hollywood. Nudie specialized in creating subtle, understated outfits of this sort for mega-successful cash 'n' flash showbiz bods. Shy and retiring Nudie drove his steer-horned Cadillac out to the movie set that Elvis was working on so that he could measure him for his togs. A fan actually nicked those glitzy gold shoelaces from Elvis's shoes. When Elvis wore this outfit for the first time he fell to his knees during his performance and annoyed Colonel Parker no end because he reckoned he'd rubbed off at least $50 worth of gold on the stage floor. So he told him not to do it again!

GI ELVIS

This is the immaculate uniform Elvis wore to return to the USA after single-handedly capturing the hearts of five or six million German girls *and* getting the monthly Best Dressed Soldier award over and over again while he was doing his military service. No matter how much muck and bullets he had to dodge, Elvis managed to remain perfectly neat and clean all the time. Elvis's spotless appearance could have been helped by the fact that: a) he used his mountains of dosh to buy hundreds of spare shirts and trousers and have dozens of extra uniforms made for him by top tailors; b) back at the house he was renting, his minders and his gran were busy polishing his boots, buttons and buckles and pressing his shirts, jackets and trousers; and c) as he wasn't living in the barracks he was able to pop home for a complete change of kit each lunchtime. See those three stripes on the arm of Elvis's coming-home outfit? That means he was a Staff Sergeant. Which he *wasn't*! Colonel 'It's Only A *Pretend* Title' Parker explained away Elvis's fictitious promotion as a slip of the tailor's needle. Ha ha ... pull the other one, Colonel ... it's got brass medals on!

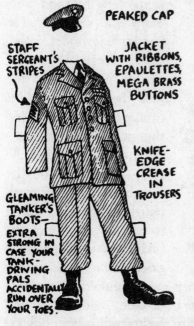

PEAKED CAP

STAFF SERGEANT'S STRIPES

JACKET WITH RIBBONS, EPAULETTES, MEGA BRASS BUTTONS

KNIFE-EDGE CREASE IN TROUSERS

GLEAMING TANKER'S BOOTS— EXTRA STRONG IN CASE YOUR TANK-DRIVING PALS ACCIDENTALLY RUN OVER YOUR TOES.

WEDDING GUEST ELVIS

Elvis wore this outfit when he was the best man at the wedding of Sonny West, his minder and brother of 'Red'.

BLACK FUR CLOTH SUIT

SHOULDER HOLSTER

BELT WITH GOLD EAGLES AND CHAINS

WHITE TIE

15" POLICE FLASHLIGHT

SECOND BELT-WITH ELVIS'S SHERIFF'S STAR AND DEPUTY NUMBER 6

BELL BOTTOM TROUSERS (EVERYONE WENT BELL BOTTOM CRAZY IN THE 1970s)

First, a word about those *two* belts. Elvis had *loads* of belts and lots of them were very *big* and very *heavy* belts. So big and so heavy that he may well have needed to wear *another* belt to stop the *first* belt causing his trousers to fall down. And the pair of hefty pearl-handled pistols that he had tucked into the waistband of his fur-cloth bell-bottoms couldn't have helped matters one bit! They were probably emergency back-up for the two guns he'd got hidden in that shoulder holster … which were obviously there in case he couldn't reach the tiny pistol he'd got tucked in the top of his boot quickly enough! *Where on earth* did he think he was going? The Last Wedding Ceremony at the OK Corral? Or perhaps he'd heard it was a 'shotgun' wedding? No one was sure why he had his police torch with him either. Actually, he'd already stuck his complimentary police-issue flashing blue light on top of the car he arrived in so it may well have been part of his carefully put together '*one wedding, two drug busts and a shoot out*' look.

BLACK LEATHER ELVIS

As you know, this outfit (which used to belong to a slightly less famous cow) was designed for Elvis to wear at that 1968 TV Comeback concert. The fashion designer who dreamed it up modelled it on a 'Levi's' denim jacket and jeans. The idea was that it was supposed to remind people of *the* young hot 'n' happenin' 1950s Elvis, which was a bit inaccurate. During the 1950s Elvis very rarely wore jeans or denim (it was James Dean and Marlon Brando who went for the tough-scruff stuff) because they reminded him of being poor and having to go to school in 'farmboy' denim overalls and get laughed at by the other kids. Now, if he'd been made to go to school in gold lamé overalls, things might have been different. Anyway, the hot TV lights and the gear and the excitement of coming back at the ancient age of 33 all got him into a right leather lather and he sweated so much that all his make-up dripped off and had to be put back on before the show even began. One rather unkind writer even said that when Elvis wore this outfit he looked like a 'human truck tyre'!

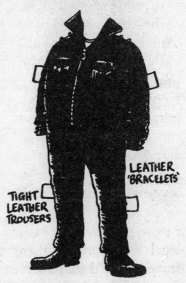

BLACK LEATHER JACKET WITH STAND-UP COLLAR

LEATHER 'BRACELETS'

TIGHT LEATHER TROUSERS

AMERICAN EAGLE ELVIS

Elvis had this restrained little ensemble knocked up for his big 1973 satellite TV-broadcast from Hawaii that was going to be watched by over a billion people around the world (and around a few other worlds too, for all we know). Because he was broadcasting to his fans all over the planet, Elvis said he wanted an outfit that would say 'America' to them all. Only days before the show, big softy Elvis gave away the mega-expensive ruby-encrusted belt and caused a right panic amongst the bods who were putting the show together because they aren't the sort of belts you can just pick up at your local Woolworth's for a fiver. The lei is a necklace of flowers that they give you in Hawaii if they like you. They didn't give him that cape though, because it cost $10,000 dollars. It was designed to twirl and whirl as Elvis cavorted around the stage. (For that sort of money it should have flown him home too.) At the end of the show Elvis took off the cape and bunged it into the audience where it was immediately grabbed by a fan. The special jumpsuit is one of hundreds that Elvis owned and wore in the 1970s. He loved his jumpsuits (so

WHITE JUMP SUIT WITH AMERICAN EAGLE MOTIF etc

RED SCARF

LEI

CAPE

RUBY STUDDED BELT

4" WIDE BELT WITH MORE EAGLES IN OVALS

homely, so practical) and was actually so fond of them that he gave them names like Red Lion, Blue Rainbow and Mad Tiger. The jumpsuits were really fond of Elvis too and showed their affection by hugging him all over so tightly that he had to wear long 'combination' undies to hide his 'panty line'. Elvis once said:

I don't think it's right for a fellow to dress loud.

On the street that is. On the stage I want to stand out. The louder my clothes the better.

PHEW!

The 'Comeback' TV special did the trick! Elvis was back in the business of making great music in front of people who loved what he did.

ELVIS PRESLEY'S REALLY BIG ADVENTURE

In 1970 Elvis was having a pretty good time being a hotshot hit again and doing regular cabaret performances at a big posh hotel in Las Vegas. But he was also feeling right upset about the state that America was in! He'd been getting himself worked up over it for a while but now he felt he just had to do *something*! He'd seen things change. Back in the 1950s, America had been all sock hops and bubble gum and apple pie and Cadillacs and wholesome fresh-faced teenagers who (very sensibly and correctly) spent their time and money screaming their bobbysox off at a brilliant, handsome young rock 'n' roller from Memphis Tennessee. Not to mention buying his records by the bucketful!

But now things had changed! The screaming teenagers of the 50s had grown up and become humdrum and boring. And the 60s peace-and-love, hippy revolution had happened! There was a new generation of crazy kids wandering around sticking flowers in odd places and wearing trousers the size of Siberia and (perhaps, *more* to the point) generally not giving two hoots about Elvis Presley and his wiggly hips!

It had never been like this when Elvis was a lad! And he didn't like it one bit! He thought that these kids and their weird ideas would be the downfall of America. The things that really bothered him about this new hippy generation were:

- They were protesting all the time, particularly about the war in Vietnam which was being fought against nasty communists by brave young American soldiers like he'd once been.

- The kids risked falling into the evil clutches of the nasty communists themselves who would brainwash them and turn them against their own country.

163

• The kids took drugs! They even *sang* about drugs. But not good, wholesome, fresh-faced drugs like the ones Elvis got from his doctors and took in increasingly large amounts. They were *illegal* drugs they bought from nasty drug-dealers in the street.

The idea of protecting his fellow citizens from wicked drug dealers and naughtiness in general appealed to Elvis no end. As a lad he'd actually thought of being a policeman, partly because he liked the uniform so much. But becoming the most famous superstar in the world had sort of got in the way of that so he had to be content with blagging badges from police forces in the places he visited and sometimes even being made an 'honorary' policeman by them. He was so proud of his collection of police badges that he had a special case made for it so he could carry it around and show it off. One day, though, Elvis met a showbiz bod who showed him a badge that made *his* badges look like a load of old Coke-bottle tops!

When the showbiz bod told Elvis he'd got his super-badge because he worked undercover for the Narcotics Bureau (the American drugs squad) Elvis knew exactly what he'd do! He'd save America from commies and drugs and hippies! And get the brillest badge in the world for doing it!

Presley's prezzie for the Presi-dent!

Just before Christmas 1970 Elvis put his drug-busting, badge-bagging scheme into action after having a bit of a barny with his dad and Priscilla over his recent rather extravagant Christmas-shopping spree. After popping out for a few prezzies Elvis had managed to come home with no fewer than ten Mercedes sports cars for the Guys *and* some stocking fillers in the shape of 20,000 dollars' worth of guns. Well, it was the season of peace and gunwill!

Anyway, Elvis was really miffed by the tiff about the prezzies so he put on his best purple cape and a super belt with a toilet-seat-sized gold buckle that those nice hotel people in Las Vegas had given him, then stormed out of Graceland and more or less jumped on the first aeroplane that came along. After toing and froing around America for a bit he eventually ended up on

another plane to Washington accompanied by his two jumbo-sized minders, Sonny West and Jerry Schilling. While they were on the plane they just happened to meet a well-known senator (American politician) who had a long chin-wag with Elvis about young people and drugs and communists and whatnot.

This chat inspired Elvis so much that he rushed back to his seat and wrote a letter. But it wasn't to Vern and Priscilla to say where he was so they wouldn't be worried.

It was to the President of the United States of America himself! In it he said things like:

> I am Elvis Presley and have Great Respect for your office.

And:

> I would love to meet you and say hello if you are not to busy....

He also said he would like to help the President to sort out all the drug abuse and communist brainwashing that was going on in America. When he got to Washington he rushed off to see a top boss at the Narcotics Bureau (Drug Busters HQ) and told him that he'd use his influence with 'the kids' to infiltrate them and suss out who was selling drugs and maybe talk to them and persuade them not to take any more drugs. So, could he *please* have one of those *brill'* badges? And the top drugs boss said, 'No way, matey!' or something like that, which made Elvis even more miffed so he stormed off to the place where the most powerful man in the world hung out. Yes, the White House, to see the President of the USA! Elvis gave his letter to the soldier on guard then felt even more cheesed off because it took absolutely ages for the bloke to recognize him.

However, not long afterwards, he got a telephone message telling him to go to the White House. This is more or less what happened next...

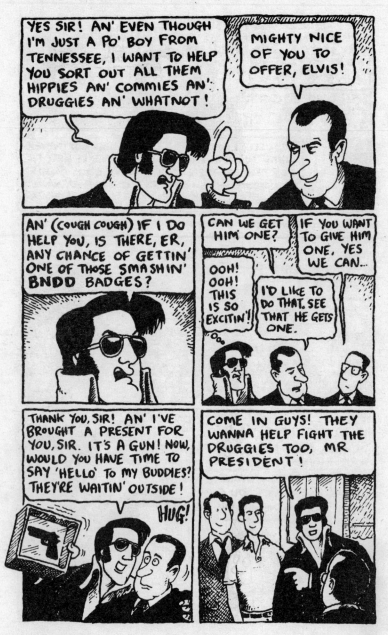

Gun Crazy

Elvis didn't just collect badges – he was also nuts about guns and spent hours 'zapping' anything that would stay still long enough for him to fill it full of lead. In addition to thinking that guns were barrels of fun, Elvis surrounded himself with weapons because he was worried about his personal safety. Ever since he'd first *shot* to fame he'd received death threats from all sorts of odd bods. Being armed to the teeth was his way of making himself feel secure. It was said that he went to bed with a gun tucked in the waistband of his silk pyjamas and kept a gun next to his plate when he ate!

• BAM! Making his big breaks in pop! When Elvis really hit the big time in the charts, he celebrated with some other pop smash hits. He lined up a thousand soft drinks bottles and blasted them to bits.

• SPLATT! Taking care of business … in a flash! Just to pass the time when they were in Hollywood Elvis and the Guys bunged hundreds of old-fashioned camera 'flash bulbs' into their hotel swimming pool. As the bulbs bobbed around on the surface they sat around the pool taking pot shots at them. With the lights turned off the bulbs exploded really spectacularly every time Elvis and his chums scored a hit.

- PING! As a way of relaxing after the strains of modern living some people have little ponds or croquet lawns in their gardens. Elvis had a firing range in his. To make it possible for him to nip out into his 'backyard' and fire away to his heart's content he had lots of human-shaped targets set up in a barn in the grounds of Graceland. A jewellery dealer once described how he'd been called to Graceland at two o'clock in the morning (an offer no sensible businessman would ever refuse) and had found Elvis out in his garden dressed in one of those long fur coats that the American pioneers used to wear blasting the stuffing out of his targets.

- BANG! Lost the remote? Oh, never mind... When the telly got up Elvis's nose he *didn't* reach for his remote control – he just reached for his gun ... and

171

shot it! Elvis is reported to have shot more tellies than other people have had hot satellite dishes. His most hated TV celebrity was a man called Robert Goulet. He was forever shooting him. But, despite having been blasted to kingdom come over and over again, for some strange reason Robert kept popping back up on Elvis's telly screens!

- KERBOOM! Car rage carnage in the garage! When Elvis got miffed with his motors he went a bit further than slamming the door in a huff – he *shot* them! He's reported to have shot several of his cars. He's once said to have gone into a fury and pumped 12 bullets into his Ferrari!
- POW! Lights out? Elvis must be here! When Elvis was staying at a hotel in the 1970s he took a pot-shot at the light switch in his room. It was a powerful gun and a flimsy hotel so the bullet went straight through the wall and into the bathroom where his girlfriend was busy doing bathroom stuff ... and screaming hysterically. During a stay at another hotel Elvis suddenly began shooting at a chandelier. The Guys got a bit alarmed and suggested this wasn't really a good idea. However, Elvis explained to them that as they were on the top floor everything would be fine as long as they shot straight up and after that they all

felt OK! One of them later excused Elvis's actions by telling a journalist that it was 'something to do', because staying in hotels was so boring.

What a pity Elvis had such a completely childish and irresponsible attitude towards guns. He really ought to have recognized what terrible things they are and not behaved in such a dangerous and careless manner. Sort of let himself down quite badly, didn't he!?

THE LAST WIGGLE

Being a mega-celeb is a glamorous life, but it's *not* an easy one! If you think that going to school's hard work just wait until you grow up and become a top rock 'n' roll star. Then you'll *really* know what hard work's all about! Elvis did more than a thousand personal appearances between 1969 and 1977. They involved thousands and thousands of miles of travelling and hundreds and hundreds of overnight stops at hotels. In addition to which, he had the constant worry of whether his performances were up to scratch and whether his fans would still like him ... or just decide he was a tubby old has-been!

And on top of all *that*, quite a few people (including some old, so-called 'friends') were beginning to say some very unpleasant things about him in books and newspapers. By 1977 he was feeling very, very tired ... and possibly even a bit fed up.

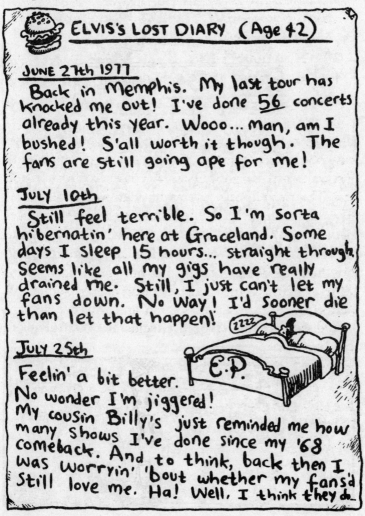

ELVIS'S LOST DIARY (Age 42)

JUNE 27th 1977

Back in Memphis. My last tour has knocked me out! I've done <u>56</u> concerts already this year. Wooo... man, am I bushed! S'all worth it though. The fans are still going ape for me!

JULY 10th

Still feel terrible. So I'm sorta hibernatin' here at Graceland. Some days I sleep 15 hours... straight through. Seems like all my gigs have really drained me. Still, I just can't let my fans down. No way! I'd sooner die than let that happen!

JULY 25th

Feelin' a bit better. No wonder I'm jiggered! My cousin Billy's just reminded me how many shows I've done since my '68 comeback. And to think, back then I was worryin' 'bout whether my fans'd still love me. Ha! Well, I think they do.

... 'cos I'm still makin' the Guinness Book of Records for sellin' more discs than anyone in the World! Yup! There's still life in this ol' Hillbilly Cat!

AUGUST 1ST

That book, ELVIS WHAT HAPPENED by Red and Sonny came out today! So angry about it I feel like I'm gonna **EXPLODE**! How could they write all that stuff about me? After all I've given them! And them my cousins too! What's worse is it's bein' serialized in the Star. The first part says I wanted to have Priscilla's boyfriend killed! **AAAAAAAAH!** I'm so riled up about it all I feel like havin' them two guys wasted. Even if they are 'family'!

AUGUST 2ND

I sent the great big Lisa Marie...

...over to California to collect the itty-bitty Lisa Marie...

Ha! And now my little girl's here to stay for a while. Ginger's niece is here too, to keep her company. As I'm writin' this, my little Lisa is tootling up and down the big Graceland drive in her mini electric golf-cart. An' her great big bodyguard's havin' to run alongside her. He's a puffin' and a pantin' while he tries to keep up with her! Ha ha ha!

HIS LAST FLAME: GINGER ALDEN

When Ginger was little her mum used to take her to stand at the gates of Graceland so they could watch Elvis ride his horse or his golf cart. When she was five he invited her to the fairground and rode the roller coaster with her. Elvis met grown-up Ginger in 1976 when he was 41 and she was a 20-year-old beauty queen. She was runner-up Miss USA, Miss Mid-South *and* Miss Traffic Safety Memphis! (She knocked him over the moment he saw her.) When she started going out with him he offered her a ride in his new Ferrari but she said it was too fast so he took her for a quick spin to Las Vegas instead … in his *jet*. The Memphis Mafia didn't like her much and called her Chicken Neck. Elvis was nuts about her though and gave her little tokens of his affection like…

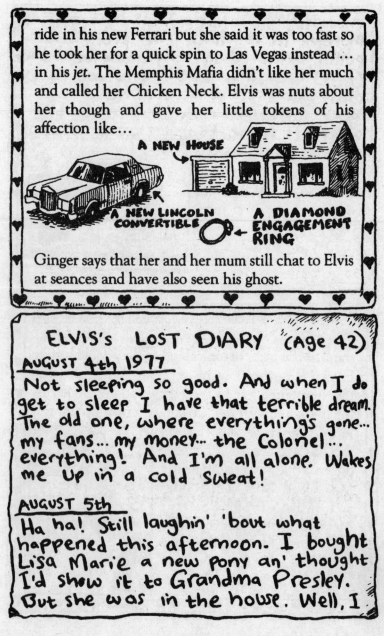

A NEW HOUSE

A NEW LINCOLN CONVERTIBLE

A DIAMOND ENGAGEMENT RING

Ginger says that her and her mum still chat to Elvis at seances and have also seen his ghost.

ELVIS's LOST DIARY (Age 42)

AUGUST 4th 1977

Not sleeping so good. And when I do get to sleep I have that terrible dream. The old one, where everything's gone… my fans… my money… the Colonel… everything! And I'm all alone. Wakes me up in a cold sweat!

AUGUST 5th

Ha ha! Still laughin' 'bout what happened this afternoon. I bought Lisa Marie a new pony an' thought I'd show it to Grandma Presley. But she was in the house. Well, I

thought, so what!... an' I just
moseyed in through the front door
pullin' that lil ol' pony along behind me.
Gave Grandma a real surprise, it did.
Only thing is, it dropped some real
good farmyard manure all over the
carpet... ha ha! Just like a scene
from lil ol' Monty Python!
Ha ha ha!

August 7th
Gingerbread said we should hire out
Libertyland (used to be the Fairgrounds)
so little Lisa and her friends could
have some fun. The kids had a
ball. I sort of had fun myself.
Left at 6.30 a.m. with the trunk of
the car just stuffed with goodies!

August 8th
Going on tour again. Colonel's already
out there organizing the gigs and
whippin' up the excitement. I hit
the road in just 8 days! Still a bit
out of shape for appearing in front of
my fans. Well, at least I've started
my 'liquids only' crash diet! Just
hope it works! Can I really lose 25lbs
in seven days? Ok! Action is better
than words. Time for a couple of minutes
on the exercise bike. Hmmm. shucks.
I could just murder a cheeseburger.

Fat's all right mama!

Elvis was a junk food junkie. The trouble was that right from when he was little, Elvis's mum had spoiled him something rotten. As she was too poor to give him goodies like toys and trips out she used her cooking skills to turn ordinary ingredients into tasty treats that had him hooked on grub for the rest of his life. And when he became wealthy he was able to spend his mountains of dosh on whatever mountains of nosh he fancied. Which turned him from a slim 21-year-old with a 32-inch waist to an 18-stone 42-year-old with a 44-inch waist. His doctor once said that trying to get him slim was 'like trying to diet a 1,500-pound elephant!'

Almost all the food Elvis loved was the stuff that's supposed to be really bad for you, like:

DOUGHNUTS, HAMBURGERS AND CHEESE-BURGERS – THE GREASIER THE BETTER.

DURING ONE SCOFFING SESSION THE NEWSPAPERS REPORTED THAT HE DEMOLISHED 8 DELUXE CHEESEBURGERS, 2 BACON, LETTUCE AND TOMATO SANDWICHES AND THREE CHOCOLATE MILKSHAKES.

Five fast-food frenzies (that are hard to swallow!)

1 Love Meat Do

Elvis loved his greasy hamburgers with the meat really well done. If a waiter brought him a hot dog or hamburger that was undercooked he liked to say, 'I didn't order me a pet!' which was his witty way of letting them know it was a bit on the raw side.

2 Cowboy fun … and a *ton* of buns

Someone once noticed that when Elvis rode his horse, Rising Sun, around the Circle G ranch he had a big, green plastic rubbish-bag tied to the saddle. It wasn't for any litter he happened to spot or to scoop poops into. It was packed full of hot-dog buns to keep Elvis fuelled up for the gruelling work of riding the range.

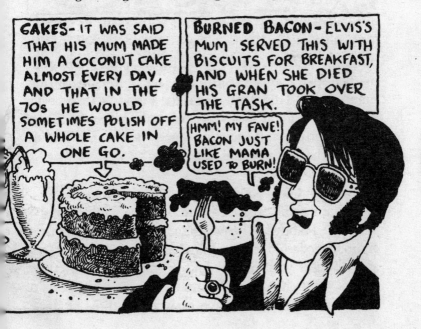

CAKES– IT WAS SAID THAT HIS MUM MADE HIM A COCONUT CAKE ALMOST EVERY DAY, AND THAT IN THE 70s HE WOULD SOMETIMES POLISH OFF A WHOLE CAKE IN ONE GO.

BURNED BACON– ELVIS'S MUM SERVED THIS WITH BISCUITS FOR BREAKFAST, AND WHEN SHE DIED HIS GRAN TOOK OVER THE TASK.

HMM! MY FAVE! BACON JUST LIKE MAMA USED TO BURN!

3 Midnight feasts

As Elvis lived a topsy-turvy life, often sleeping through the day and staying up all night, he was subject to more than the average amount of nocturnal snack attacks. However he didn't have to sneak down to the fridge to pig out on leftovers like normal gluttons do because his kitchen staff were on 24-hour stand-by to rustle him up a lil ol' midnight feast whenever he felt like one.

ACTION STATIONS! SCRAMBLE! SCRAMBLE! FRY! FRY! THE KING'S FEELIN' PECKISH!

4 'In yer face' food

Sometimes, when Elvis and the Guys were having din dins, one of them would suddenly scoop up a dollop of mashed spud and smear it in the face of the Guy sitting next to him. This was a signal for a food fight to begin and in no time at all everyone would be pelting peas, lobbing lettuce and squirting sauce. However, it was all done in the best possible taste.

5 Just nipping out for a takeaway

When Elvis did a concert in Denver, Colorado, he discovered sandwich heaven at a restaurant which made giant super-sarnies by scooping out the middle of a loaf and filling it with peanut butter, grape jelly and crispy bacon. Back home in Memphis he suddenly got an uncontrollable urge to have him one or three of these

'Fool's Gold' monsters, as they were called. Without hesitation he phoned an order through to Denver, saddled up his private jet, rounded up some of the Guys and then flew half-way across America to pick up his take-out order of 22 giant sandwiches!

Elvis's Fried Peanut Butter and Banana Sandwich

These are a sort of 'Fool's Gold' for beginners. They were Elvis's favourites to rustle up in the kitchen at home and are strongly recommended for weight-conscious people (those who want a bit more). Eat as many as you like and see the pounds shift (from the kitchen cupboard to your waistline).

What you need:
Some rich, creamy peanut butter. (Anything between one jar and several wheelbarrowloads will do – depends on how peckish you're feeling.)
Some bananas, extra ripe.
Some slices of buttered bread.
Some butter.
A frying pan.
A knife or spatula.
Some paper towels.
A large plastic bucket.

What to do:
Mash up the bananas and the peanut butter until it's a big gooey mess. Make your goo sandwiches. Put the rest of the butter in the frying pan and when it's completely melted and sizzling drop in the sandwiches. After a couple of minutes turn them over. When they're nice

183

and golden remove them from the pan and drain them on paper towels. OK! They're done. Scrumptious or what!

Serving suggestion:
Get at least three tellies and install them in your bedroom. (Elvis liked to watch in triplicate.) Cover your windows with tin foil. (Elvis's minders did this so he could pretend day was night.) Now slip on your monogrammed silk pyjamas, get into bed and pig out on tons of telly 'n' tuck.

Wake up sometime later feeling absolutely terrible. OK! Where's that bucket?

All that lot's not exactly what you'd call a healthy diet, is it!? Which is probably why Elvis ended up in hospital a few times during the 1970s for various sorts of stomach problems and whatnot. And in addition to being a junk food addict he was now taking absolutely tons of drugs, all prescribed by his doctor in order to help him sleep and slim and relax. No wonder he was feeling under the weather!

ELVIS'S LOST DIARY (Age 42)

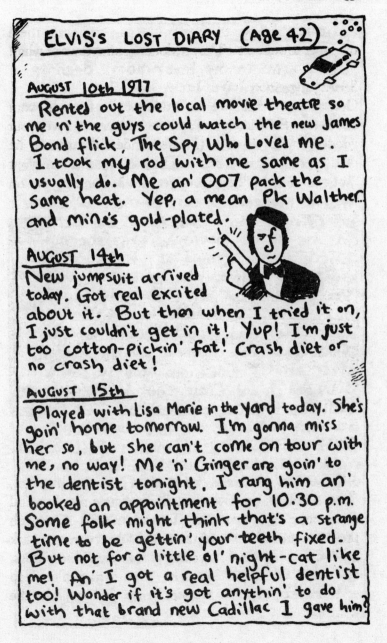

AUGUST 10th 1977

Rented out the local movie theatre so me 'n' the guys could watch the new James Bond flick, The Spy Who Loved Me. I took my rod with me same as I usually do. Me an' 007 pack the same heat. Yep, a mean PK Walther... and mine's gold-plated.

AUGUST 14th

New jumpsuit arrived today. Got real excited about it. But then when I tried it on, I just couldn't get in it! Yup! I'm just too cotton-pickin' fat! Crash diet or no crash diet!

AUGUST 15th

Played with Lisa Marie in the yard today. She's goin' home tomorrow. I'm gonna miss her so, but she can't come on tour with me, no way! Me 'n' Ginger are goin' to the dentist tonight. I rang him an' booked an appointment for 10.30 p.m. Some folk might think that's a strange time to be gettin' your teeth fixed. But not for a little ol' night-cat like me! An' I got a real helpful dentist too! Wonder if it's got anythin' to do with that brand new Cadillac I gave him?

185

AUGUST 16th

It's about ten in the morning and I'm sittin' in my bathroom. Been up the whole night long but I'm still having a bit of a problem gettin' to sleep. An' some stomach pains (pesky diet!) I'm still thinkin' about what happened earlier. It was just a simple little thing but it reminded me of how much my fans mean to me. When me an' Ginger got back from the dentist in the small hours of this mornin' there was a crowd of them around the gate (just like usual). We stopped the car an' this lady stood next to me and held her little girl up so her daddy could take our photo. That was real nice an' touchin'. Well, after that I felt kinda good so I got Billy and Jo and Ginger out on the racquetball court for a knockabout. All that activity has wore me out some but I still ain't sleepy! Ginger's fast asleep right now. Lucky her! I told her I was comin' in here to read. But I ain't! I'm writin' up this li'l ol' private diary. And just as soon as I'm finished I'm gonna stash it in its secret hidin' place. Wonder if anyone will ever get to read it when I'm gone? Actually, right now, not feelin' too good...

THE NATIONAL INTERFERER

SPECIAL EDITION　　　**AUGUST 17th 1977**

ELVIS PRESLEY IS DEAD!

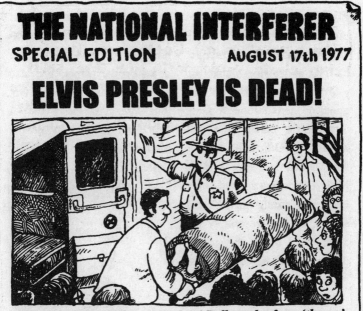

·World in shock as King of Rock 'n' Roll topples from 'throne'

THE KING'S LAST NAP
by Perry Pry

Yesterday I attended a news conference at which it was announced that Elvis Presley, the King of Rock and Roll, is thought to have died sometime between nine o'clock yesterday morning and two in the afternoon. His girlfriend, Miss Ginger Alden, found him slumped face down on the carpet of his bathroom at 2.15 p.m. She called his bodyguards and doctor who summoned the local paramedics. Elvis was rushed to hospital but was pronounced dead on arrival.

Elvis had been up all the previous night visiting his dentist and playing racquet ball. At about nine o'clock he told Miss Alden that he was going to the bathroom to read, to which she replied 'Don't fall asleep!' so he said 'OK, I won't!' (his last ever words). Miss Alden awoke some hours later and seeing that Elvis's side of the bed was empty she assumed that he was downstairs or elsewhere, so she made a phone call to her mum. After this she shouted to him and on receiving no reply she entered the bathroom and was horrified to find Elvis face down on the carpet. She also saw that he had been sick. Not long after this the whole of Graceland erupted in terrible screams and groans!

THE FAN'S LAST SNAP
by Sam Snoop

I have just spoken to a Mr R Call, who was standing at the gates of Graceland with his wife and daughter when Elvis returned from that late-night trip to the dentist.

'It was after midnight,' Mr Call told me. 'Me and my wife had made a special trip up here from Indiana with our little daughter Abby so we could get some family photos of us all in front of Graceland. Imagine our surprise and delight when none other than the King himself pulled up in his car. Straight away my wife lifted little Abby to his window and he just did this great big grin and waved. What a great guy he is, sorry ... was!' When I put it to Mr Call that he had probably taken the last-ever living photo of the King of Rock 'n' Roll he just looked shocked and said, 'You don't say. Well, shoooot!'

ELVIS'S FUNERAL

10PM: 1 HOUR AFTER ANNOUNCEMENT OF ELVIS'S DEATH: CROWD OF 1,000

MIDNIGHT: CROWD OF 3,000

NEXT DAY: MILE LONG QUEUE OF 20,000 FANS

END OF DAY: 75,000 PEOPLE ATTEMPTING TO PAY RESPECTS

THE FUNERAL

THE ELVIS EFFECT

When Elvis performed, thousands of normally quiet, well-behaved people instantly became raving nutcases. And it wasn't just because they were *teenagers*! Wiggle Hips even drove 'wrinklies' (i.e. people over 20) completely nuts. It was reported that when Elvis was wowing 'em in Las Vegas in the 1970s, grown-up women dressed in glamorous evening gowns would suddenly leap out of their seats and rampage across the tables to get at him, treading in people's dinners and spearing steaks with their stiletto heels. The way Elvis drove audiences crazy was really extraordinary. Even his regular backing band never ceased to be amazed by it. Looking back on it all years later Elvis's lead guitarist, Scotty Moore, remembered how he'd seen a whole hall full of people almost 'explode' when Elvis did 'Heartbreak Hotel' and thought to himself 'What *is* going on here?' People who witnessed Elvis the Pelvis mesmerizing thousands of fans said it was as if he transmitted a sort of invisible power – almost as if electricity passed from his body to theirs (ooer … shocking!).

Elvis himself was a bit gobsmacked about his effect on fans. He once said to his band, 'I bet I could burp and make them squeal.' So he did, and guess what happened!

Ever since Elvis got famous people have been imitating his style. Some did it by copying his hairdo and clothes. Check out all those grandads who were teenagers in the 1950s and notice how they desperately cling on to their ancient Elvis Presley quiffs.

Others did it by going the whole hog and becoming Elvis Presley impersonators. There are now thousands of them all over the world, including carol-singing Elvii and even a team of sky-diving Elvii! One man even had plastic surgery so that he could look just like Elvis. But there's no need for you to go for drastic plastic to look Elvtastic. Just follow these simple instructions and you'll be a wow!

How to be an Elvis impersonator

The following instructions are for the 1956 version of Elvis (there are loads of people copying the 1970s model already). However, if you do wish to add a touch of late model Elvis to your performance, there are a few handy tips towards the end.

What you need:

• Hordes of devoted fans. If you can't find 10,000 screaming 1950s-style American teenagers to strut your stuff in front of you'll just have to make do. Maybe with an ex-1950s teenager like your gran. Or perhaps with someone who screams at the drop of a rattle like your baby brother or sister? Or maybe even the family pet...

• An absolutely stunning wardrobe. You'll need some groovy 1950s gear. Go back to 'Welcome to my wardrobe(s)' (p. 153) for ideas.

• A microphone. The old-fashioned sort, not one of these titchy modern things that you hardly notice, and you'll need a stand with a lead trailing from it. A broomstick with a bit of string attached will do. Elvis used to get so passionate with his mikes that he sometimes broke them in two.

• Something to chew. Elvis often chewed gum while he sang. Not an easy thing to do – you could easily get it wrapped around your tonsils and choke to death mid-wiggle.

Why not chew something more easily digestible like a poptart or a cheeseburger! But avoid spraying your audience with half-chewed quarter-pounder!

• A full-length mirror. When young Elvis was preparing himself for his really important gigs he spent hours practising his famous wiggles and sneers in front of a mirror.

• Several gallons of sweat. Elvis put tons of energy into his act and sweated buckets. However, the perspiration wasn't all down to his high-octane wiggling. Elvis had noticed how gallons of sweat gushed off one of his own heroes, rhythm and blues singer Jackie Wilson. Jackie told him that he took a load of salt tablets and drank a couple of lakesful of water before he went on stage and that 'the chicks' really dug his dynamic dripping. So Elvis, that other 'big drip', copied this idea. This is an amazingly DANGEROUS thing to do as it can cause a fatal heart attack! DO NOT try it yourself! Just rely on leaping about to create your pondful of perspiration.

OK, you're ready. Now's your big moment. They're all out there waiting for you. They've booed so viciously that the poor little girl playing the xylophone has rushed off the stage in tears and they've chanted, 'We Want Elvis! We Want Elvis!' so noisily and insistently that the corny old comedian has walked off in disgust. These things actually happened at Elvis's early concerts. In those days rock 'n' roll gigs often had support acts like acrobats, magicians and jugglers! Now listen! Your fans are in a frenzy of expectation. You can't let them down. The consequences could be horrible!

All this stuff came completely naturally to Elvis. His second manager, Bob Neal, said that when Elv was on stage...

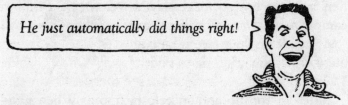

He just automatically did things right!

Well, it may have come easy for him. But are *you* up to the Elvis challenge? We'll see!

195

What to do to wiggle your way to fame and fortune:

1 Walk out on to the stage. You've got to get the walk 'right'! It's no good trotting out like you're receiving 'swot-of-the-week' award in Friday's school assembly. So ... don't meander snootily ... saunter moodily! Someone once described Elvis's walk as a cross between a slouch, a mince and an amble. Well ... that must be a slinble? *OK ... y'all, SLINBLE!*

2 Look your audience in the eyes (not easy when your eyes are outnumbered by at least ten thousand to two). Now ... *sneer!*

No, not like you *hate* them! Elvis *loved* his fans! Make it more of a cheeky, playful sneer. Allow your sneer to frolic around your lips ... then let your lips go for a playful scamper around your cheeks.

My goodness your face *is* having fun! OK ... now it's time to pout!

3 Curl your top lip and sneer a bit more. When Elvis studied the movies of top stars Marlon Brando and James Dean he worked out that they hadn't got where they were by just grinning like extremely gormless Chesire cats. If you feel a smile or giggle coming on, turn your back on the audience and put your hand over your mouth (or just put your head in a paper bag).

4 Strum your guitar a couple of times. Elvis wasn't one of the greatest instrumentalists in rock 'n' roll ... but that's not the point. Being *too* good at playing your instrument can sometimes get in the way of producing a blistering, raw, hard-hitting, monster pop performance. In fact, some of the most successful musicians in pop have what is known as 'limited technical ability' (i.e. they're useless).

5 It's almost time to get into some serious 'body language'! Just leave your guitar dangling around your neck like an oversized bit of wooden jewellery. But here's an important tip. Someone said that Elvis 'read' his audience as he performed. And if he saw them respond  to his sneers and pouts and twitches and wiggles he 'gave them a little more'. Like an extra wiggle ... or a bonus-points pout. So, if *your* fans are beginning to react to *you*, maybe it's time to lob them that half-eaten pop tart?

6 Now for some fancy fingerwork. Spread your arms and 'flutter' your fingers like you're paying 'air piano' … like an 'air guitar' but much heavier. By the way, don't forget to keep sneering! And remember to keep your wrists nice and limp, like a rag doll.

Imagine you're 'feeling your way along a wet walled underground passageway'. That's actually how one magazine described Elvis's movements back in the 1950s.

Actually, at this point, it might be quite nice to let your mouth hang open a bit. So, let your bottom lip droop like wet underwear on a washing line. Lovely! Oops, watch out … you're dribbling all down your gold lamé jacket. Better shut it again, quickly!

7 Get on down with some real smoochy microphone action! Grip your microphone … like it was the most handsome boy/beautiful girl/cuddliest stick insect you've ever held, snogged, chatted up or used as a snooker cue.

198

Now, fall on your knees and sort of bend over it like you're going to give it the smooching of its lifetime! Hey! Stop that this minute! You don't know where that broomstick's been.

Listen! You don't actually have to *kiss* your microphone. Just drag it around the stage a bit.

8 Kick-start the leg'endary 'Elvis the Pelvis' limb action. If you're doing your stuff successfully your fans should be going quite crazy at this point. So now's the time to hit 'em with everything you've got and get the famous leg joints jumpin'! Start by jerking your left leg about a bit. OK! Put your right fist in the air and give your hips a couple of shakes. Now ... 'snap' your legs with the lethal Elvis the Pelvis 'jack-knife' action!

No, not like that! That's a scissor kick! One more of them and you'll be up in the rafters (or out in the car park). You've got to snap and waggle your legs with a sort of hopping, skipping, jerking, shuffling action that

moves you backwards and forwards across the stage.
Brilliant! Much better. Oops!

OK, not to worry, climb back on to the stage and try to
look where you're going next time. Now, as a sort of
finishing touch, you must sharply *swivel* a leg, then drag
it around behind you like it's not feeling too good. Oh
yes, nearly forgot! You have to stay on tiptoes with your
knees pushed as far forward as they'll go through at least
80% of this section!

9 Collapse! This will floor your fans ... and *you*! Drop on
to your knees at the front of the stage then put your head
in the lighting trough.

When Elvis did this the screams of his fans nearly took the roof off. (Perhaps it was *his* screams too, when his hair began to smoulder?)

If you haven't got a lighting trough, the dog's bowl will do. Now for your '*coup de grâce*' (that's French for 'chew the grass'). If you're performing on an outdoor stage jump off it then fall on all fours and begin to 'gnaw' the grass. If you're indoors, you'll just have to nibble the carpet. Elvis once did this at a football stadium gig while he was singing 'You Ain't Nothing But A Hound Dog!' He leapt from the stage, then began to chew the turf like an over-excited Shetland Pony. It drove the fans wild.

10 Freeeeeze! This'll be a good moment to use some of those 1970s moves we mentioned. Hopefully they'll quieten everyone down. Before the fans can start stealing your shirt buttons, climb back on to the stage. (What do you mean your mouth's full of carpet fluff? You weren't *really* supposed to gnaw it!) Anyway, your song's about to finish. During his cabaret period Elvis was fond of freezing in a sort of statue-like 'pose' at the end of each number. So if you've ever played musical statues you'll know exactly what to do. When the music stops ... just FREEZE!

Brilliant. Perhaps Elvis was hoping his fans would join in the fun and try and spot him twitching or smirking. One rather unkind writer thought Elvis's various freeze poses looked rather silly and decided to give them all names like ...

ELVIS THE GLADIATOR

ELVIS THE DISCUS-HURLER

ELVIS THE DYING GAUL

Right, you're done; you're now a fully qualified Elvis Impersonator. All you've got to do now is put that lot to music. Why not try 'Blue Suede Shoes', 'All Shook Up' (or 'Away In A Manger'). And don't forget, if you do decide to become an Elvis clone ... it could make you rich. Some of them earn as much as $15,000 a week!

AFTER ELVIS

Elvis fans may have been devastated by his unexpected death but that didn't stop them worshipping the King and enjoying his brilliant music as much as they'd ever done! Perhaps even *more* than they'd ever done?! During the months after he died, Presleymania seemed to get bigger than ever! Between 1977 and 1980, despite the fact that he was off doing the great rock 'n' roll gig in the sky, Elvis still earned *more* money than any living entertainer.

The king is dead ... long live the king

- After Elvis died his fans rushed out and bought *twenty million* of his records ... all in one day!

- Tons of new Elvis merchandise hit the shops, including bottles of Elvis's sweat, and Elvis Presley toilet seats! (But the fans complained they kept falling off them.)

- A man bought Elvis's old ranch in Mississippi and began selling seven-inch-long bits of the fence to his fans. People who bought the bits of wood got a certificate signed by Elvis's cousin, Billy, to say they were the real thing.

This is a bit of our old coffee table genuine piece of wood from ELVIS'S RANCH FENCE signed: Billy Presley

- Graceland was opened as a tourist attraction in 1982. Elvis is buried there next to the swimming pool, alongside Gladys, Vernon and Grandma Minnie.

It's the second-most visited house in America (after the White House) and about a million Elvis fans still go there every year. The 10-mile stretch of Highway 51 that runs past Graceland had already been renamed Elvis Presley Boulevard in 1972 (after which Elvis was given two coats of tarmac and had double yellow lines painted across his bottom).

- In January 1983 the American Post Office issued a stamp with a really nice picture of Elvis on it. Here's what *some* crafty Elvis fans did with the stamp. They  invented an address which they hoped wouldn't exist then sent a letter to it with the Elvis stamp on. The US mail would then return the letter to the fan who posted it because they couldn't find the house. The envelope would now be stamped 'Return To Sender – Address Unknown', which was the title (and first line) of Elvis's million-selling 1962 hit single!

- Another big Elvis tourist-attraction is the Shotgun Shack in East Tupelo. It was first opened to visitors in 1971 by Elvis's old teacher, Miss Grimes. Some Elvis fans even go there to get married. In 1979 the area around it was renamed Elvis Presley Heights.

- Elvis fans still regularly meet at enormous Elvis gatherings known as 'conventions'. Sometimes as many as 100,000 of them get together so they can talk about Elvis, listen to his records and watch Elvis impersonators.

- In 1986 over 200 Elvis impersonators appeared at a birthday party for the Statue of Liberty.

- On 8 January, 1993 1,200 Elvis impersonators appeared in 50 states across America to celebrate what would have been Elvis's 58th birthday! (No wonder some people think he's still alive!)
- Yes… some people reckon Elvis is still alive and that he faked his death so that he could do undercover anti-drugs work for the FBI. There are regular reports of him being spotted all over the place. He's often seen working in supermarkets in glamorous places like Wigan and Pittsburg. Check out your local hyperstore, but if you do spot him … keep an eye on your junk food!

• Since he died more than 400 books have been written about Elvis and his music! Which is ridiculous! No matter how famous and amazing someone is, that amount of books is *completely* over the top. Anyone writing another ought to have their head tested!